THE BOYS OF
NORTHWOOD

By
Randy Mixter

ISBN-10: 1475250177
ISBN-13: 978-1475250176

By Randy Mixter

Swan Loch
Sarah Of The Moon
Letters From Long Binh: Memoirs
of a Military Policeman in Vietnam

CONTENTS

INTRODUCTION

The stories gathered in these pages are for the most part true. One or two have been given the benefit of a fertile imagination. A few others were casualties of a memory that tends to become more forgetful as it ages.

You may notice that the stories stray from a chronological order. I might be eleven in one tale, then sixteen in the next. Followed by a story in which I'm a pre-teen again. Some of the narratives encompass more than one event or a particular time frame. After an attempt to follow a timeline, I concluded that the stories should stay, much like my life in those days, unorganized.

Though several of the short tales are from my perspective, I tried to put the burden (or in some cases the blame) on my fellow Northwooders. These stories are really about them. Some have passed away, but we all live in these pages. The Northwooders will always endure in the stories we tell.

If you happened to be young in this wild yet innocent time, you might find similarities in these stories to your own adolescence. If not, then this is what you missed.

HALLOWEEN

One of the many good things about growing up in a row home, or townhouse as they're called today, was that on Halloween night there was very little walking to do between front doors. If one had the ambition to jog or avoid the sidewalks and cut across yards, two full shopping bags of candy by nights end would not be out of the question.

The Northwooders had Halloween down to a science. A few days before the event, we would gather around the dining room table and map out a strategy. We would note the houses that, the previous year, had been generous with their handouts. We would also note and cross off the 'apples' and 'pennies' homes. Any establishment that made us do a trick for our food also faced elimination.

Our gang was serious when it came to candy. Most of us received maybe five dollars a week allowance, of which at least half of it went to candy. A good Halloween would give you up to two full weeks of the stuff. That meant more money for comics and baseball cards.

In our neighborhood, the more enterprising in our group actually went out the night before Halloween to try their luck. Believe it or not, a few people did give out candy on that night, probably just to get rid of us.

I must note that I don't remember ever wearing a costume on Halloween. Perhaps during my childhood my parents made me wear something silly, but by the time I went out on my own, it was strictly casual wear. It was the same thing with my brother and our friends. No one in our gang would have been caught dead in a costume. One could certainly argue however that our manner of dress back then was costume enough.

As we entered our teen years, Halloween became less about treats and more about tricks.

Moving night (the night before Halloween) in Northwood was an occasion most adults feared. True to its name, lots of stuff got moved on moving night. Backyards, in particular, suffered the most during this tradition. Our standing philosophy was that if an item wasn't locked down or too heavy, it would be moved. Trashcans were usually the first to go, but chairs and small tables were popular too. We avoided lawn ornaments such as flamingos and gnomes. They were considered too creepy.

Usually these items would just go into the next yard. If a neighbor were to give us grief during the year, the items more than likely would go missing. The woods near our home became a haven for such yard decor. I have no doubt there are raccoons still calling those rusty '60s trashcans home.

Our gang would also not above utilizing a tried and true classic; the burning bag of dog poop by the front door. Every Halloween we did this gag. I can't remember a time when it didn't work, even if it was multiple times at the same residence.

I recall one moving night where we wandered a few blocks out of our neighborhood. We came across a house with a foot high picket fence around its perimeter. Thinking it would be easy pickings, I began to pull the little wooden posts out of the ground. I was about halfway through when the front door of the house flew open. The four of us took off running. Let me say up front that I was a fast little guy back then (I was maybe 13 at the time).

Anyhow, we were running along at an impressive clip confident that we'd made a clean getaway. I seem to recall something attaching itself to my back. I looked down at my feet. They were still going a mile a minute but they weren't touching the pavement. Just as disturbing was the fact that I appeared to be about a foot in the air.

It seemed that the owner of the property, a man who I guessed to be in his mid thirties, had in fact caught up with me. Me! The fastest kid in the neighborhood had been outrun by a middle-aged adult.

He had grabbed me by the back of my belt. Once I was securely in his grip, and my feet had stopped flailing about, he calmly turned around and carried me back to his house.

By this time, my friends had stopped and watched in amused amazement as this angry homeowner walked me up the block. Because he had me by the belt, I dangled from his arm like a turtle out of its shell. I was too frightened to attempt escape. I simply swung about watching the sidewalk pass beneath my eyes.

When we finally arrived at his house, he walked over to where his little picket fence had fallen and, without saying a word, held me there over it. After a few seconds, I got the hint and began to put up the fence while still a couple of feet off the ground.

At some point, when I was about halfway through my landscaping, I caught a glimpse of my buddies. They were across the street in the throes of wild convulsive laughter. Then, just when I thought things could not any more humiliating, the guy's daughter stepped on to the front porch. Though I could only catch her face on the upswing, she appeared to be my age and quite cute. Despite my predicament, I attempted to introduce myself, only to hear a gruff "shut up!" from above my head. It was the only time I heard my captor speak, but it was loud enough to shut me up. I was wise enough to assume that I didn't stand much of a chance with that girl anyway.

After constructing the picket fence to the man's satisfaction, he took me to the curb and dropped me to the ground. Then, without looking back, he walked into his house, closing the door behind him.

I wobbled to my feet, tightened my belt by a notch and then quickly got out of there. I was traumatized enough to think that the guy might decide he had some inside repairs for which I could be of use.

The gang never let me live that incident down, and, as for me, I had learned my lesson. On future Halloweens, I only wore beltless pants.

PORCHING

Let's not mince words. Porching was the fine art of taking someone's beer for your own personal consumption. That the 'someone' was usually one's neighbor, made the act even more reprehensible. But we did it anyway because, damn it, it was free beer. In the 1960s (and long before) many homeowners would find that they lacked adequate storage for their beer and malt liquor purchases. Wives in those days, and today too I guess, frowned on beer cans using up their limited refrigerator room. Fridges were smaller then and barely held the necessities such as milk and Royal Crown soda. The refrigerator in my house was simply a cold space for leftovers. Leftovers stayed in my fridge long after the memory of the original meal had faded.

The first week of each month would be fresh home-cooked meals. The following three weeks would be the leftovers of those meals. At the end of the month, my mother emptied the fridge and the cycle restarted. I sometimes think, looking back on it, that there was a store somewhere that sold strictly leftovers at reduced prices, because I swear that more than once I was eating food that my mother never cooked.

In our house, only two beers at any given time were allowed in the fridge. The remaining beer had to be hidden in a relatively cool spot within the house. Our basement had a small secured ashbin in the concrete wall directly beneath the living room fireplace. During the warmer months of the year, it became the perfect hiding place for my father's stash.

Of course, my brother and I found it. It turned out we had the same idea, but my father beat us to it. We ended up hiding our ill-gotten liquor in the woods by our house. The problem was that by the weekend we would forget under which rock we put the stuff. I'm telling you, it was rough enjoying a beer in the '60s.

The winter months were a different story however. Then you could simply put your beer supply on the back porch and let Mother Nature take care of the refrigeration. In Northwood, practically every home was part of a row of connected houses whose backyards faced alleys.

Unlike today, there were no decks out back and no gas grills. During the summer, backyards were used for hanging wet clothes on lines and possibly tending a small garden. The yards were too small for much else. Back porches were tiny cast iron things that provided quick access to the alleys. If you wanted to socialize with the neighbors, you'd hang out on the larger concrete front porch. The rear porch was good for one thing only: beer storage.

To add to their charm, wives and mothers never went out back during the cold months. My mother in particular would often forget we even had a rear house entrance. Sometimes in February, I would catch her staring at the back door as if it were a foreign object.

The main reason any of the teenagers in my neighborhood looked forward to the wintertime (besides snow days) was we could finally drink cold beer. The problem was getting it.

The art of porching beer was not for the faint of heart or the weak of mind. I personally witnessed many a teenager give in to their desire for a 'cold one' only to be caught by an irate neighbor or, worst yet, the police.

The concept of porching was simple enough. One or two guys would be appointed as porchers on any non-school night. Any more than two would look suspicious. The designated porchers would walk the dark neighborhood alleys glancing at back porches as they did so. The first target was always beer cans or bottles, but brown bags and cardboard boxes would also be scrutinized.

Upon observing an object fitting that description, a practiced porcher would always walk past the house to map a strategy. Inexperienced porchers who 'jumped the fence' at this juncture usually paid a stiff price for their haste. Many a porcher would abandon their fellow 'jumper' when the porch light came on and all hell broke loose.

After mapping out a proper strategy, the actual porching would commence. Things happened quickly at this stage. It was an unwritten law that if you couldn't hop the fence, grab the stuff, hand it off, then hop the fence again in under 10 seconds, you were probably going to be unsuccessful.

Greed also played a part in failed missions. Young and foolish porchers would sometimes try to jump-start their reputation by grabbing a case of beer. Big mistake! Experienced porchers knew to go light and fast and take no more than two six packs at a time. One six-pack was the best bet. More often than not, the resident never realized it was missing.

Even good porchers were waylaid from time to time. I remember one party where we sent out our best porcher and all he came back with was a dead goose. He excitedly swore that it had some use, but our group could find none. He was made to take it back to its final resting place while we reluctantly filled ourselves on Coca-Cola.

The most extreme instance of porching, to my recollection, was my friend Jimmy who porched a case of beer from his next door neighbor in broad daylight. One minute our gang was in his back yard eyeing the case, the next minute it was in his hands on our side of the fence. His quickness was such that no one had even seen him commit the act.

If there was ever a porching hall of fame, Jimmy's name would certainly be there.

SUMMER SCHOOL

When a student at our high school screwed up and failed some of his courses, his options were limited. He might be held back a year, or he could end up in summer school.

Here is the way it worked. If you flunked one subject, you were safe, and moved on to the next grade. If you failed two courses, then summer school was in your future. Three or more failures and you'd be repeating the grade.

Let me tell you this upfront, nobody in the school system, teachers and administration, wanted a kid to repeat a year. My 'all male' high school wanted its students to absorb as much knowledge as possible during their four year stint, then gracefully exit, and *please* don't come back unless asked.

A student hanging around and repeating years meant that some young man who really wanted to learn couldn't get in the door and had to enroll in the vocational school down the street.

My high school had a two-flunk policy. They would let you fail two years, then after that, no matter how bad your grades, they would graduate you. They wanted you out of there before you became of drinking age.

Of course, you would not be allowed on stage during the graduation ceremony. They were ashamed of you after all. They would place you in the rear of the auditorium, usually the last row. The lights back there were turned off so you wouldn't be seen, and when they called your name you were not allowed to stand. You could wave as long as it was for two seconds or less and your hand was not higher than your forehead. Then your diploma was passed back to you by the people in attendance.

The preferred method of punishment was summer school.

Summer school began almost immediately after school broke for summer vacation. The school did not want to give a student time to access the summer vacation mentality. Another reason for the early start was to get it over with before the dog days of summer began. As in some classrooms today, there was no air-conditioning. Even with a fan and open windows, the rooms were uncomfortably hot.

Though the classes were held during morning hours, the oppressive heat made it impossible to study. Everyone, including the teachers, became lethargic. The teachers in particular had problems with the heat. Whether they were there for the extra money, or if they too were being punished, was beside the point. Most were as miserable as the students. If you were fortunate enough to be in one of those classes where the teacher simply gave up, your class assignment would often be 'catching up on lost sleep'.

Sometimes, however, the heat would serve to further infuriate an already angry instructor. I once heard of a classroom of students required to perform, along with their normal studies, at least twenty pushups daily.

To make matters worse, sometimes summer classes did not take place in your old familiar school. Maybe the school custodians didn't want to spend a part of their quiet months unlocking doors for rowdy pupils. Or perhaps it was determined that the classrooms failed to approach the prescribed oven like conditions. It was not unusual to receive a letter a day or two before your first class stating that you were now to attend a school that was a little closer to the equator.

Summer school lasted about a month. By mid-July, it was just a bad memory. There was no real anticipation about receiving your grades because nobody ever failed summer school. No matter how bad your grades, if you attended regularly, and lost at least a pound or two of sweat-induced weight, you passed.

Some crafty teens used their summer school experience as an excuse not to find a seasonal job. They would tell their parents that now, in the middle of July, everything was taken. Most parents did not fall for this ploy and sent their wayward son straight to the local moving and storage warehouse that was always hiring. A few parents, perhaps thankful that their sibling had made it through another school year, took the bait, and subsequently gave their teen a free pass for the remainder of the summer.

Anyone who has been through summer school will tell you that, no matter what your teacher's disposition, it is not a lot of fun. Usually a round of summer school would put a student on the straight and narrow path. That was the goal of summer school. If your mind absorbed anything during those weeks, it was sheer luck. Summer school was punishment, pure and simple. If you learned your lesson, and actually studied a bit the next school year, then the school had accomplished its task, and most likely already had a chair reserved for you in the dark last row of the auditorium.

WATCHING TELEVISION

Let me start by saying I did not watch much daytime TV in the 1960s. After school I would sometimes watch The Buddy Deane Show, The locally televised dance show was the inspiration for the Hairspray movies and musical. The show was segregated, so most of the time white teenagers danced with other white teenagers. Occasionally a recording artist, looking to promote a song, would come on the show and do some bad lip-syncing.

Every so often the blacks would take to the dance floor. On those days a white person was nowhere to be found. Even Buddy Deane hit the road. Those were also the shows with the best dancing.

Now the fifties were another story, what with The Howdy Doody Show and Disney's The Mickey Mouse Club.

But my goal from the time I became a teenager (I was thirteen in 1960), until I went into the army in 1966 was simple, spend as much time outside of my house as possible.

I guess that my friends shared the same philosophy, because we'd always get together after school for some play time before supper. Very rarely did I have to call one of my buddies to get together. That was a good thing because we had a party line on our phone and the woman we shared our line with had numerous medical ailments to discuss with her friends in the afternoons.

After my parents divorced in the late 50s, my brother and I were told to spend Monday through Friday afternoon with my father. My mother would have us from Friday evening through Sunday were spent with my mother. Fortunately for us, my mother only moved six blocks away, so we made a new set of friends along with the old ones.

Occasionally all our friends from both communities (we were separated by woods) would get together and either fight or play.

Anyhow, my mother enforced a strict curfew on our Friday and Saturday nights, so my brother and I would stretch out on the floor in front of the fourteen inch black and white television and watch TV until we were told to go to bed.

We were not allowed any food or drink in the living room, while we watched, because my mother had a white shag carpet there. A plastic runner ran from the front door to the dining room. My brother and I were under strict orders not to walk on the carpet and to stay on the runner. That did not make a lot of sense to me since we had to take our shoes off upon entering the house. Were our socks that dirty? In addition, when we watched television off the runner, we had to put on our pajamas. Even our clothing was not good enough for that white carpet. Our friends, once they heard the carpet horror stories, wanted no part of that living room. When they did come over, they stayed mostly in the basement.

To the best of my recollection, some of the shows we watched on Friday and Saturday nights were: 77 Sunset Strip, Bonanza, My Three Sons, The Flintstones, The

Twilight Zone, Route 66, Maverick, Cheyenne, Sugarfoot (at some point they alternated these three), and I think Hawaiian Eye and Surfside Six.

Those were the shows I watched with regularity. The others that I watched pretty much all the time were (and I know some of these are '50s shows) The Adventures of Superman, The Adventures of Ozzie and Harriet, Leave it to Beaver, Wagon Train, Boris Karloff's Thriller, The Dick Van Dyke Show, The Many Loves of Dobie Gillis, Lassie, I Spy, The Man From Uncle, The Wild, Wild West, Adventures in Paradise, and The Untouchables.

Later on, after I returned from Vietnam, I enjoyed Rowan and Martin's Laugh-In, The Mod Squad, and The Smothers Brothers Comedy Hour. Other than those, I can't recall watching too many other series. I do recall watching The Honeymooners on a small black and white set in New Jersey in the winter of '68 and thinking it was the funniest thing I'd ever seen. But my wife and I had just gotten married, and I had better things to do.

It was a good decade for television, which, much like me, was a youngster too. I didn't savor it as I should have because I was young and impatient, and was easily seduced by the fresh air beyond the front door. But I do remember those weekend nights on the white carpet, mesmerized by the boob tube.

PARKING

If you were a teenage boy in the 1960s, and fortunate enough to have both a car and a girlfriend, you might be one of the lucky few who experienced the unique thrill of parking.

Parking, in simple terms, was the act of a guy and a girl making out in a vehicle parked in a secluded area under the stars.

In those days, getting intimate with your girlfriend in your house was frowned upon by even the most liberal of parents. I didn't have a single friend with the courage to French kiss or lay hands on their girlfriend in any home when parents were lurking about.

Do not let anyone tell you any different, fathers, in particular, knew when their daughters were being touched. My girlfriend's father seemed to have a sixth sense when that type of activity was occurring somewhere in his house.

My girlfriend's dad didn't like me much to begin with. He would get mad if I even glanced his daughter's way. Yet she would insist that her basement was safe at night, that her parents were sound asleep two floors up. But, without fail, the minute we'd sit on the sofa, I'd begin to hear noises. I would put my arm around her and the noises increased. It sounded as is someone was attempting to walk quietly across the hardwood floors and failing miserably.

My girlfriend would swear it was only the house settling, but I knew better. I knew that the second our lips met, her father would appear on the steps. He'd have a crazed look about him, and be carrying an axe or a shotgun.

I would plead with her, once the strange noises began, that her father would say in court that I molested her. This would be his defense for my murder. My girlfriend would call me a wimp and laugh it off, but I didn't care. I was sure I was playing into his diabolical plan to rid her of me.

Taking a girl out to park in your car was not an easy task. Most girls were reluctant to do it. There were a couple of reasons for this. One was that girls were not as afraid of parents catching them as guys were. They correctly knew that all fathers, and most mothers, would blame the boyfriend for the transgression. They were safe no matter what, and they had a bathroom and refrigerator close by.

Another reason was that guys liked to park in dark quiet spots off the beaten path. This maneuver had a logical enough reason. Teenagers did not like other teenagers watching them through the car windows. You could not rely on the windows fogging up. Sometimes, despite one's best efforts, they just didn't.

That is why drive-in movies were only used in a pinch. There were just too many people walking around the cars. It made no difference where you parked in a drive-in theater. Before the night was over, someone would be looking into your car.

Girls did not like dark lonely spots. Rest assured that if you talked your date into parking on a dirt road in a wooded area, you would be sternly reminded of crazed men, with hooks instead of hands, prowling in the darkness. She would tell you things you did not know, such as the mental institution, with lax security, a short distance away, and the civil war graveyard just past the tree line.

It would not take long for these stories to take root. Perhaps a tree branch scraping the vehicle's roof would add urgency to her words.

On those nights, a drive-in, with its curious inhabitants, didn't seem like a bad idea. However, if you could somehow convince your skeptical date that no harm would befall her in such a peaceful pastoral setting, then you could finally park in earnest.

Truthfully, nothing particularly sordid ever happened while parking. Second base was about as far as any young man got back then. If one were to tempt fate and try to round third, one would find that, no matter what your watch said, it was getting late and time to go home.

Besides the threat of mental institution escapees, you always had to be on the lookout for cops. Most let you alone, but a few would bother you. They were usually the ones upset at working the late shift on a Saturday night, or perhaps they had a teenaged daughter and were playing the odds. Whatever the reason, a flashlight shining into your car invariably spelled trouble.

When this happened, it was best to quickly button up, smooth down your hair, and have a quizzical look on your face. More often than not, if you were sober and apologetic, the cop would simply send you on your way. Sometimes, if the officer was in a playful mood, he would address your date as if she were a familiar figure in those surroundings, asking her why she was back again so soon and, by the way, who's that guy you're with now.

Despite the many distractions, parking was one of the few alternatives to celibacy back then. Our options were limited and parents were on the warpath. On top of that we were, like most teenagers today, quite horny. We made do with what was available.

Cars were large and roomy with long vinyl seats and lots of space to spread out. They were living rooms with a steering wheel. With the possible exception of the Volkswagen, they were made for making out. It was such a popular endeavor that at a local reservoir on any given Saturday night there would be as many as a hundred or more cars with foggy windows lining its roads.

But as vehicles got smaller and parents became more open minded, and maybe slept a bit more soundly, parking became a lost art.

My girlfriend and I did eventually marry and till this day she is adamant that, despite what the police officer said, I was the only one she ever parked with.

I'LL MEETCHA AT AMECHE'S

In the late 1950s and the 1960s, drive-ins meant two things; a place where you could go eat (but mostly drive around and try to pick up girls), or a place where you could take in a movie (but mostly make out with your girlfriend).

Let's start off with the drive-ins that served food and drink. A drive-in named Ameche's was located a few short miles up the road from Northwood. It was named after, and I believe owned by, the great Baltimore Colts player Alan Ameche. Their slogan was 'I'll Meetcha at Ameche's'. I remember that because I still have one of their ashtrays.

Ameche's had booths for inside eating, but, for the teenagers of the time, the preferred method of dining was outside, in one of the drive-in slots.

Most of the cruising car drivers would not pull into one of the many drive-up stalls for one simple reason.....you had to buy something once there. Ordering a soda wouldn't cut it. Food of some sort needed to be purchased also. You had to make it worthwhile for the waitress to risk life and limb walking among the inattentive young drivers.

Once in the space, an irritable, and barely understandable, mechanized voice would demand your order. If you hadn't made up your mind, or just simply couldn't read the condiment splattered menu, you were out of luck. After a few short seconds, the robotic voice would assume you were broke and just parking to save gas. It would tell you in a loud shrill manner to immediately vacate the space or else. The threat was disturbing enough to send many a driver quickly out into the traffic flow without care of vehicle damage or bodily harm.

There was also the problem of tipping. The Northwooders could usually scrape together enough change for a burger and a drink, but we never had anything left over to give to someone for bringing us food. Most of the female servers accepted this fact and just took their time with our orders as our penance. But non-tippers did run the risk of further antagonizing an already hostile hostess. It was common knowledge that if a carhop recognized you as a cheapskate and offered to hand you your milkshake, there would be an unfortunate accident involving clothing and the car seat.

I have to point out right off the bat that the young women who worked at Ameche's, unlike their movie counterparts, did not wear roller skates. The fact of the matter was that they often spilled their food trays by simply walking with them. I imagine that if they wore roller skates, the food and drink loss alone would have been astronomical, not to mention the money paid out for injury and property damage lawsuits.

Luckily, most of the teenagers hanging out at Ameche's did not do it for the food. However, in all honesty, I rather enjoyed their 'Powerhouse' burger. Like most hangouts back then, the guys were there to meet girls, and the girls were there to meet guys.

The layout was such that, if you were fortunate enough to have a car (usually your parent's), you could spend hours cruising around the building and its adjoining drive-in area.

I seem to remember the unfortunate few without transportation being relegated to a curb that separated Ameche's from a Ken's Big Boy restaurant. There, they would stand and watch the parade of cars pass by. Occasionally someone would spot a friend driving around and, if the driver had neglected to lock his doors, hop in with him. Keep in mind that this person did not have to be a close friend or even a distant one. I recall that on at least one occasion I hopped into the car of a complete stranger. Desperation drives one to extremes.

I don't recall ever picking up a girl at Ameche's drive-in, which I guess defeated the purpose of going there to begin with. I think it was because when I did manage to secure a vehicle it usually was my father's light green 1958 Chevy station wagon. Not a real chick magnet. But I would like to think that even the guys driving Mustangs weren't having much luck either.

Ameche's went the way of most drive-ins of the 1960s. It was still around when I joined the Army in July of 1966, but by the time I got out in 1969, it was gone. The intersection, as of this writing, houses a Rite-Aid Pharmacy.

WEAPONS OF NOT SO MASS DESTRUCTION

The boys of Northwood were nothing if not pranksters. Of the many ways we'd find to humiliate our friends, the worst, by far, was the water balloon.

During any hot summer day, it was advisable to be wary of a possible water balloon attack. These acts of violence would usually occur at random, and could originate from any makeshift hiding place.

If there was a sure thing in our neighborhood, it was this. If you were walking alone down an alleyway on a warm and sunny day, perhaps searching for your friends, and you noticed it was quiet, too quiet, then it was too late. Your fate had been decided. You were going to be the victim of a water balloon attack.

Already, in an upper level bedroom, an arsenal had been prepared. Balloons of different sizes were filled and ready. The least filled smaller balloons were more accurate and subsequently used for distance tossing. The larger heavier balloons were made for close impact, usually when the person was directly underneath you or opposite your hideout.

A well-coordinated water balloon attack assured that the victim would receive a thorough soaking from head to toe. Extra credit was given when the deflated balloon shreds stayed on the clothing and off the street.

Sometimes the soaked victim would yell an obscenity or two and run home to his mother, but usually the young man would take the soaking in stride, knowing that, with the possible exception of his socks and tennis shoes, the sun would soon dry his clothes.

More often than not, the sneak attack would provoke an all out war. Sides would be chosen, more balloons would be filled, and the back alley would shortly thereafter become a man-made river.

Though strategies were mapped out with a military-like precision, the balloon battles, after a while, always became sloppy close contact affairs. Once you were soaking wet, you really didn't have much to lose. Any individual, young or old, who, during the heat of conflict, decided to use the alley as a shortcut, or take out the trash, was fair game.

I can personally think of at least two occasions when an innocent homeowner took a balloon just for being in the wrong place at the wrong time. I remember that the Mister Softee man also took one for the team one particularly violent afternoon.

Another type of weapon was the peashooter. Plastic peashooters were cheap but lousy for distance. For a little more money, one could purchase a metal shooter that not only guaranteed a longer range but also increased accuracy.

Peas were no problem. Someone's parents always had a bag of them lying around the house. They were rarely missed and, if the bag was full, supplied a week's worth of ammo.

Pea shooting was not without its dangers. Usually we'd use some rusty cans or bottles as targets and keep score based on direct hits. But sometimes old grudges between participants flared up at inopportune moments and peas would hit flesh.

When this happened, any boy wearing glasses had a distinct advantage. A pea would sting the face or limb at close range, but one in the eye would certainly put you out of commission for a spell. The mouth was another place you didn't want a pea. The realization that the pea in your mouth was a second earlier on the tongue of your buddy was reason enough to quickly make for the nearest hose and engage in a long thorough rinsing.

Slingshots were also popular in our group. Much like the peashooter, they were used for target practice. Small rocks and pebbles were popular projectiles, but every so often we would place a cracker ball in their canvas pouch.

Cracker balls were tiny round paper wads with a little bit of gunpowder inside. When tossed onto a hard surface they would make a noise of about the same volume as a small firecracker. Cracker balls were fun to use where a few people gathered. I recollect bus stops as being a popular cracker ball locale.

When used in a slingshot against a can, the little ball could do considerable damage. Some of the more daring shooters would put five or six of them in the slingshot's pouch, affectively creating a poor man's shotgun.

We were barely intelligent enough to know not to aim a slingshot in the direction of each other, but that didn't stop us from shooting around unsuspecting feet to provoke scares and strange dance moves.

Lastly, some of us found that by taking a springed clothespin apart and reassembling it, we could create what we liked to call a match gun.

A wooden match would be placed in the mouth of the makeshift gun. These were called safety matches. How they got that name, I will never know, since they would light on pretty much any dry surface. Some of our gang would even show off and light them on their pants zippers, though I was never brave enough to try that.

If the day was hot enough and the sun bright, safety matches would sometimes simply give up and light without any provocation. We all knew better than to carry any around in our pockets, they were simply too unpredictable.

Once the wooden match was in the makeshift barrel, you would give it a squeeze. The match would fly out and ignite against the first object it touched. If a match was put head first into the clothes pin, it would ignite immediately.

We were always careful to use our clothespin guns in the safe concrete confines of the street and alley, and never used them when any adults were nearby. We learned our lesson with the Mister Softee man and the water balloon. He avoided our alley for the rest of the summer after that incident and we certainly did not want to lose the Good Humor man too.

SHIRTS WITH TABS AND OTHER CLOTHING

In the early sixties, there were two lifestyles that affected your clothing choices. On one side you had the greasers (or birds, as we called them), still holding on to their '50s fashion choices: leather jackets, upturned shirt collar, skintight sharkskin pants, pointy black shoes, and cigarette pack folded into the white undershirt sleeve.

Then, on the other side of the spectrum, you had the more conservative dressers (or squirrels, as the greasers called us). We wore button down shirts, khaki pants and jeans, and tennis shoes or loafers. There were really no in-betweens back then. You were either a bird or a squirrel, period.

Our gang was comprised strictly of squirrels. Anyone who wandered into our neighborhood with pointed shoes, or cigarettes in their sleeve, would have been politely told that they were on the wrong side of town. Not that they wouldn't have known it. Occasionally a few of us would ride our bikes a few miles away to a section of Baltimore called Hampden. I knew the area well because I was born there.

We liked Hampden because the main drag, 36th Street, had a neat movie theater (I remember seeing *The Mole People* there), a used comic book store (I think it was in someone's basement) where you could buy comics for as little as two for a nickel (yeah, they were a little beat up, but who cared), The street also held a drug store with a large soda fountain, and a five and dime. It was a nice place to visit but, unfortunately, Hampden in the early 1960s was infested with birds.

We were always a little concerned when we visited that part of Baltimore. We just did not know how the birds would react to our squirrel invasion. But we need not have worried, they were always polite and tolerated our presence. We never took the chance of overstaying our welcome, however. There was always an underlying feeling of dread that at any time our button down shirts or Jack Purcell tennis shoes could set one of them off. We saw our movie, bought our comics, and then got the hell out of there.

There were two Ivy League stores a short drive from our neighborhood where we bought most of our shirts and pants, Frank Leonard's, and The Oxford Shop. The problem was that they were rather expensive. A cheaper alternative was The Sample Store in Waverly near the great old Memorial Stadium. There you could buy factory reject shirts and pants, similar to the expensive retailers, at discount prices.

They were fine for the most part. The shirts sometimes had a button slightly off-center or a small bleach stain or two. The pants might have a leg a half-inch shorter than the other, or a stubborn zipper. Other than that, they were okay.

The girls liked the shirts because they had a thin one inch long tab between the shoulder blades on the back of the shirt. I guess the tab was sewn on the shirt for the convenience of hanging it up, but most girls just could not wait to walk up behind you, put a finger through the tab and yank it off. If you were lucky it didn't rip the shirt. Girls simply loved to do this and collect the tabs. I guess it was a status thing for them. The more tabs, the more powerful the hunter. I knew one girl who had over one hundred tabs. She was avoided on a regular basis.

Looking back on it, I don't know why we just didn't cut off the tabs with scissors right after we bought the shirts. Maybe we just liked the attention.

Bleeding madras was also a sought out shirt style in those days. It was not popular with mothers, however. Despite their best efforts, the shirts would always manage to find their way into a washing machine where, in the midst of white dress shirts and blouses, they lived up to their name.

Because of the constant wear and tear, and the fact that our parents paid for them, we bought shoes as often as possible. On the tennis shoe side, I would alternate between Hummers and Jack Purcells. They were the tennis shoes of choice in our gang. For casual shoes, I once again took turns between taffy penny loafers (they had the sewn on lumps on the sides) and Bass Weejun loafers. For dress, I liked scotch grains and wing tips. We also wore shoes called desert boots, which were tan suede high-tops, and sort of a cross between dress shoes and sneakers.

Jackets and coats also took a beating back then. Not necessarily a bad thing considering that every year a new style of jacket or winter coat would become popular.

The most popular jacket in the early '60s was the flag jacket. It was a standard lightweight jacket with large rectangular red, white, and blue stripes running across its front. There were different varieties and patterns of these color combinations to break the monotony. My favorite was a cheaper offshoot of the flag jacket worn by at least one guy in our neighborhood. The front of that jacket featured colored Xs and Os. I don't know which country's flags they represented, but they were widely mocked by the true flag jacket wearers, and the Xs and Os made good target practice for water balloons, pea shooters, and slingshots.

There were several popular winter coat styles. The reversible parka, the oxford suede, the herring bone/glen plaid reversible, and the lawman were favorites. I preferred the glen plaid reversible, while some of my friends preferred the lawman. For me, the glen plaid was like having two coats in one, and I would often reverse it many times in the course of a day.

In those years wearing a coat envied by others could be problematic in the sense that eventually one of your buddies would get it from you either by an ill conceived bet or careless neglect.

A good coat would likely change hands many times over the course of a single winter before, hopefully, ending up back in the hands of its rightful owner.

Unlike the '70s, the styles back then were pretty cool, and some, like the button down shirts with tabs in the back, still exist today. If only my wife would stop yanking those damn tabs off.

BASEBALL, FOOTBALL, AND PINKIES

During the last week of school before summer vacation, when homework had become a distant memory, a large chunk of our afternoons and evenings were devoted to preparation for the baseball season. Up until that point our weekends mostly consisted of alley handball. The Northwooders played baseball on the two nearby fields at Northwood Elementary School and, while school was in session, the teachers and administrators frowned on anyone using their fields. Even on weekends, they would leave a surly janitor behind to do their dirty work.

We could never understand their obsession with their ball fields. For one thing, the students never played on them. Their recreational time was spent in a fenced in asphalt area where dodgeball reigned supreme. For another thing, we never saw anyone play on those fields. Truthfully, they were not well maintained. The infield was more stones and pebbles than dirt. In the outfield, grass had long since conceded the turf to weeds and other less recognizable vegetation.

The debris littering the ground gave our infielders a good lesson in heroism. Hard hit ground balls seemed to have a mind of their own as they bounced erratically across the rocky surface. Black eyes and split lips were a common sight for anyone brave enough to play shortstop or third base.

The outfield wasn't much better. Many a good running catch was circumvented by a tangled mass of undergrowth that lived for the taste of tennis shoes.

Yet the school staff protected these run down killing fields to a man. Thankfully, when the students left for the summer so did the teaching and administrative staff. I seem to recall some even sneaking out before the final bell rang. What had been sacred ground a short week before was now a 'do whatever you want, break a leg, we don't care' piece of property.

So, in the final week of school, we'd soak our gloves in buckets of oil, scrounge around for last year's hardballs (nobody played softball back then), and dig up unbroken bats.

The first few games of the summer were always cause for celebration. All the neighborhood kids would turn out. We frequently had such a huge gathering that many a mediocre player would be forced to sit the game out, unless he was willing to bribe the team captain with a healthy portion of his weekly allowance. As the days passed and the injuries mounted, the enthusiasm waned. By mid-summer, ball games with as few as three guys on a side, and team captains begging for money, were not uncommon.

We played many games with just a pitcher, a first baseman, and an outfielder. The pitcher would cover home plate on well-hit balls. The first baseman would run ahead of the batter on balls hit to the outfield, hoping for a tag out.

If you were batting at the plate and your fellow players were on base, you would have to retrieve the ball after every errant pitch. There were no calling balls and strikes in our games. You simply swung at decent pitches until you either hit the ball or struck out.

If there was but one outfielder, the batter would have to call the field where he thought he was hitting the ball. In this regard I was hated for being a left-hander, because the outfielder would always have to move to the opposite field when I batted, then back again for the right-handers. Suffice to say, when we played baseball shorthanded, everyone got a lot of exercise.

We played handball on the summer days when we were too lazy to walk to the school. Handball could be played in the alley by our homes, and all you needed was a pinkie to play.

A pinkie resembled a tennis ball stripped of its canvas cover. They were popular for alley play because they rarely broke windows. Someone in our gang always carried a pinkie on his person at all times. It was an unwritten law. Though the pinkie person was always popular on nice days, it was also somewhat embarrassing to be carrying one around. They tended to create a large bulge in tight cut-off jeans pockets. Pinkies were multi-purpose balls that could also be used for wallball and stepball.

Handball was played in much the same manner as baseball. Bases would be designated in the alley and then the fielding team would spread out as much as possible in those narrow confines. The hitter would toss the ball in the air then swing at it with his fist. Any ball hit into a yard was an automatic out. A caught ground ball or fly ball was also an out. If you hit a car or pedestrian, you were also out.

Most of the neighbors were tolerant of pinkies landing in their yards. The majority of them had kids and understood. One of the neighbors, however, hated us to the extent that she would try to grab any round object that fell on her property. When a pinkie crossed that fence it was usually a mad scramble as to who would possess ownership, the fielder or the homeowner. Thank goodness she was a slow elderly lady. Most of the time the ball was back in our hands before she was halfway across her yard. But even with her poor success ratio, she would often prowl that backyard like a Willy Mays want-to-be, hoping for that perfect catch.

Stepball was a game that needed to be played on weekday afternoons because the playing field was where there would normally be parked cars. The only thing one needed for stepball, besides the pinkie, was a few concrete steps on the front of a row home. Because the front of the house my brother Steve and I lived in was sloped and fit the criteria. Our front steps were often used in our stepball games.

There were no teams in stepball. It was all individual effort. The person with the pinkie would stand in front the steps while the other players would line the street. The objective was to throw the pinkie against the steps. Two caught grounders were an out, as was a caught fly ball. Most throws resulted in the ball hopping into the air for an easy out. If you were lucky enough to pitch the pinkie at such a precise angle where it hit the apex of the step, the ball would shoot off the concrete like a rocket, almost always resulting in a home run.

Since there were no bases to run in stepball, the only hazards were in the field where players were apt to collide with parked, and sometimes moving, vehicles.

Football was reserved for the cooler autumn months. Once again we played at the elementary school, but on the open field in front of the school property where the ground was grassy and soft. Soft was important because we always played tackle without benefit of padding of any sort. In fact, in warmer weather, we often played barefoot.

The janitor who worked the occasional weekend became a major obstacle in our enjoyment of the game. I imagine the custodian became upset each time he witnessed our group destroying his well-manicured front lawn.

He rarely mustered up the energy to confront us. Instead, he would think of other diabolical ways to force us off the grounds. One time, unbeknownst to us, he scattered the grass with thumbtacks. I can only assume he must have seen us playing barefooted. I am certain he chuckled from his vantage point at a classroom window as we excitingly ran out on to the field that cool November morning.

The tacks, and the subsequent foot injuries, gave us reason to wear footgear, but we still neglected padding. We never held anything back and the games were rather brutal affairs. No one ever got killed, but there were plenty of bloody noses and sprains, and every once in awhile a tack would need to be removed from a players butt.

HIGH SCHOOL DAYS

Let me start by saying I went to an all male high school. There were a number of public high schools that separated the boys and girls back then. My high school, Baltimore City College, had been doing it since 1928, a long time to keep horny teenagers apart.

Next to the school, but separated by a street, was Eastern High School, a school for girls. There was a rumor floating around the entire time I attended the City College that an underground tunnel existed connecting the two schools. To my knowledge, no student ever found that tunnel, though some were lost in the attempt.

Due to the number of students attending City College, we were put on shifts. The first shift was from 8 am until noon, for juniors and seniors. Freshmen and sophomores went from noon until 4 pm.

I remember the first and second year students complaining, to any one who would listen, about starting classes so late in the day (this shifting started in my junior year so I avoided it). I can't say I blame them. It was a hell of a thing to sleep in, eat some breakfast, watch some television, and basically get a goof-off mood firmly established, then realize you had four hours of school ahead of you.

I was lucky enough in my junior and senior year to acquire a friend named Dave who owned a car. It wasn't much of one, an old blue Volkswagen Beetle, but it had four wheels and an engine and got us from point A to point B.

Occasionally we would hook school, which seems ridiculous when I think back on it. I mean we did get off at noon. You would have thought we could have handled those four morning hours.

The reason we cut school was very arbitrary. We would sit in the school parking lot and listen to music on the beetle's AM radio until the last possible minute and make a mad dash for homeroom.

If the song 'Homeward Bound' by Simon and Garfunkel came on the radio during this wait period, we would cut school. It was as simple as that. Of course, there were other days when we just simply didn't want to go to school when pretty much any song would do. I seem to remember cutting once when 'Exodus' by Ferrante and Teicher came on.

The weird thing about our cutting classes is we'd usually end up in a place designed to educate. More than once, we traveled to The Smithsonian Institute and other museums in Washington, D.C. At other times, we would end up in the public library reading books.

Our classes, after a ten minute homeroom (what was the purpose of homeroom anyway), were divided up into forty minute segments. You had five minutes between each class to hurry outside and grab a quick smoke.

There were no girls to impress, so the classes themselves were relatively quiet. Being boys, occasional pranks livened things up throughout the day. We never messed with the teachers though. They were a serious bunch who wouldn't hesitate to show you detention. I believe there was some heavy drinking going on after-hours with a few of those instructors. They always seemed hung over and short tempered.

I must tell you the worst possible punishment a humorless teacher could inflict on a rowdy student. Before the shifts went into effect at our school, our school cafeteria was bustling with activity between the hours of 10 am and 1 pm, when lunch was served. A student who was considered a troublemaker (yep, that was me sometimes) would be given trashcan duty for a week.

Trashcan duty went like this. For forty-five minutes at lunchtime, for a full week, you would walk around the crowded cafeteria pushing a large trashcan on wheels. In theory, your fellow students would walk up to your can, as you passed them, and deposit their trash in it. In fact, they never did that. What they would do is use your trash can as target practice. The good students would use your can to practice their passing accuracy. The bad students would aim at you. Believe me when I say that at my high school bad students far outnumbered the good.

Baltimore City College still stands today (I believe its co-ed now), perched high on a hill overlooking the city. A reminder of times good and bad, and trashcans on wheels.

SWIMMING POOLS AND SWIMMING HOLES

The Northwooders was fortunate enough to have two great places to swim within driving distance of my neighborhood. One was a quarry; the other, a public swimming pool.

Much like today, many communities on the fringes of Baltimore City had private community pools. We, as a group, avoided those establishments even though we had one within walking distance of our homes. They were simply too hard to sneak into. A ten-foot fence that was topped by coils of barbed wire surrounded the community pool closest to us. My army compound in Vietnam was not as well fortified. Even though it meant we had to pay an entrance fee, we settled on the public pool or the quarry.

The quarry was the more dangerous of the two. Despite the best efforts of the management and the lifeguards, there were always a few near drowning deaths and other mishaps during any given summer. I don't remember much else about the quarry. Our gang really didn't go there that often. The ambulances idling in the parking lot dissuaded us.

The welcome alternative was the public pool in Baltimore County. It was a short drive from our neighborhood but, because most of our swimming

44

occurred on summer weekdays, we relied primarily on our thumbs to get us there and back.

Once there, we would change from our cutoff jeans into our cutoff jean swimsuits. No Northwooder had a normal bathing suit back then. They were either considered too sissified or just not cool, I'm not sure which.

The pool itself was huge and comprised of mostly shallow water. It started about six inches deep (there was no wading pool for the tots) and worked its way down to a ten foot diving area. There was a large fenced-in grassy area, for spreading out your towels, surrounding the pool. There were even a couple of trees in the back of the expanse that provided 'make out' privacy for the lucky few.

Unless we were showing off for girls, we stayed off the diving board and away from the deep area. Our favorite water game was tag, in which the person who was 'it' tried to tag another person so they could be 'it'. Nobody wanted to be 'it'. No wonder. Once you were 'it', you were avoided like the plague. Even the older family swimmers, not playing the game, avoided you. It was quite demeaning to be 'it', and if you were stuck in that capacity for any length of time, rest assured, therapy was in your future.

We would do whatever it took to avoid being tagged by the person who was 'it'. That might include grabbing an innocent child to be used as a shield if near capture.

I also remember diving in extremely shallow water (the lifeguards let you, if you were dumb enough to do it). My brother and my friends did this also. Looking back on it, it's a wonder any of us made it through those days relatively intact.

There was one summer that was particularly memorable, more for the music than anything else. It was the summer of 1964 and three songs played repeatedly on the jukebox in a small pavilion by the pool. The songs were 'Don't Worry Baby', 'I Get Around', both by The Beach Boys, and 'Fingertips Pt. 2' by Little Stevie Wonder.

'Don't Worry Baby' got the most airplay. In the summer of '64, at The Orchards Swim Club, it was the song of choice. Thank God, it was a great song.

That public pool also had dances occasionally on Friday nights during the summer. There one could dance to live music in the pavilion and, of course make out by the trees in the moonlit grass.

A few years ago, my brother and I and our wives, drove up there to see if the pool was still around. We found that the entire area was now an industrial park. It was the same fate that met our drive-in movie theater. But I could swear, as we were pulling away, I heard the final chords of 'Don't Worry Baby' faintly drifting on an August breeze.

THE GREATEST SUMMER JOB EVER

I had three summer jobs during the 1960s. Two were so bad that I'd just as soon not discuss them. One, however, was a great job that I had in the summer of 1965.

Hutzler's Department Store was getting ready to open a retail outlet in a county outside of Baltimore. They had a warehouse in the heart of the city in an old three-story building. It was there, in the summer of '65, that they stocked their merchandise for the autumn opening at their new location.

I can't recall how I found out that they were hiring stock boys at that warehouse. I do remember the interview process being a breeze. The supervisor doing the interviews checked my pulse to see if I had one, then hired me. I started work in the early part of July, eight in the morning until five at night with a one-hour break for lunch. On my first day, they put me to work on the second floor with another teenager around my age who had been there for a couple of weeks.

As I soon discovered, it was a lucky break landing on the second floor. The first floor was a madhouse of activity. All the bosses worked on that floor, as well as many clerk types sorting and separating merchandise. There was a lot of yelling on that floor, due to a lethal mix of pissed-off supervisors and incompetent employees. The second floor, by comparison, was a quiet slice of Eden.

My job was to assist the other guy in stacking and doing inventory on the boxes arriving by freight elevator. We would get anywhere from twenty to a hundred boxes a day. The normal daily average was around fifty or so. The guy I worked with had the counting and stacking down to a science. On an average, we worked maybe two or three hours a day.

My co-worker had also been crafty enough to stack some of the box piles with secret entrances and small caves. I found out my first day there, when he disappeared for short intervals, that he was using the caves for napping.

The third floor was also used for counting and stacking boxes. The ground floor crew sent the smaller boxes up there. The reason for the smaller boxes was that three teenage girls worked the third floor.

Of course, being guys, we were thrilled when we discovered girls working on the floor above us. We would sometimes trek up there and do some innocent flirting. But more often than not, we would sneak up the stairs and scare them. Or we would hide behind boxes and engage the girls in rubber band battles. Those were innocent times.

At lunchtime, we would walk to the building next door where they had a snack room. One unique feature of this area was a separate long narrow room. This room was dark and had a long line of comfortable lounge chairs of different sizes and shapes running down its left wall. A tired worker would simply pick an unoccupied chair and catch a nap. A couple of minutes before the end of the hour, someone would open the door and flicker the lights to alert us. Many a day I'd quickly chow down my bagged lunch to grab an available chair.

The second floor of the warehouse was also long and narrow. We would stack the boxes on both sides of the floor, leaving a walkway down its center. At the end of the floor was a small stairway that connected our floor with the first. Next to the stairway was the freight elevator.

At some point, after I had been on the job a few weeks, my co-worker and I began to get restless. I mean one can only take so many naps in the course of a day. Our floor had a container on wheels that we used to transport boxes to their appropriate stack. The container was around four feet across and five feet long. It was open at the top with canvas sides. One day, out of sheer boredom, we decided to give each other rides in it. We would start at the far end of the hallway. One of us would get in the canvas and the other would give the container a running push and a good spin. The person in the cart would fly down the aisle, bouncing off the boxes on its perimeters, until finally coming to rest at the far end by the staircase.

The word of our fun ride somehow filtered down to some of the teenaged employees on the first floor. Soon, on any given day, there was a line of kids waiting their turn on the contraption.

As luck would have it, tragedy eventually reared its ugly head. I remember helping a first floor employee into the container. My second floor buddy gave the wheeled contraption a particularly vicious spin. The youngster swiftly sped down the corridor, careening off the boxes. His speed was such that he barely slowed down at the corridor's end. He angled off one last box stack and then proceeded to bounce down the stairs to the busy first floor. The guys on our floor witnessed this event in awestruck horror. Then we scattered. The first floorers flew to other parts of the building, my friend and I retreated to the safety of our caves.

We found out later in the day that the teenager was shook up, but otherwise fine. In fact, he had the presence of mind to tell the first floor bosses that he had fallen into the container while helping us unload some boxes near the steps. Just to be on the safe side, the rides stopped after that.

Towards the end of August, the first floor supervisors got everybody together and told us that, starting the next day, we would be loading boxes into trucks for transport to the new store.

If memory serves, just about all the young employees, myself included, quit on the spot. It certainly was a great job while it lasted.

RECORD HOPS

In the late 1950s, and until their demise around the mid '60s, record hops were the place to go on a Friday or Saturday night. You could hear good music being played loudly on a 45-rpm record player and, as an added attraction, girls were present. In fact, if one was unfortunate enough to attend an all boys school, record hops were the best place to meet members of the opposite sex.

I first started going to record hops in the '50s. The elementary school a couple blocks from my house had one every Saturday night in their gymnasium. They called it the Northwood Rec. I'm sure they had no choice but to put it in a gym. But a gym smells of old sweat socks naturally. The odor seeps into the floor and walls and cannot be removed by any means. On top of this, in order to keep the floor scuff-free, we had to remove our shoes upon entering. The Northwood Rec was, without a doubt, one smelly room.

Back then we didn't mind the smell much. It was a small price to pay for the entertainment. My brother and I actually met some of our best friends at that record hop.

Most of my friends, and I'll include my brother and I, were cheap as could be. Any money we couldn't extract from our parents we'd try to bum from either other our buddies or complete strangers. We weren't proud, and some of us would go to reckless, even dangerous means, to save a buck (or in most cases less).

The following is the story of how my brother met one of our closest friends.

Steve and I were preparing to enter the Rec from the second floor entrance. Ahead of us was the table where the fifty-cent entrance fee and shoes were collected. As I approached the table, two quarters in hand, I noticed that Steve had gone missing. Assuming he'd forgotten something at home, I paid my fifty cents, gave up my shoes, and entered the dance hall. Several minutes later, and about halfway through 'Tequila' by The Champs, Steve appeared in the dance hall. He seemed in good spirits though his clothes were a wrinkled mess. He had a young man with him that I'd never seen before. Steve introduced the teenager as Jon, and then related the following story of their meeting.

According to my brother, Jon was in the second floor bathroom relieving himself when he heard a commotion at the open bathroom window, twenty feet above the school grounds. He turned and was shocked to see a face staring in at him. The face proceeded to politely ask him for a helping hand.

Jon quickly completed his business, and then went to the daredevils aid. The mountaineer was my brother, who for the want of saving fifty cents, had risked life and limb climbing up the school wall by means of an old rainspout.

Jon helped him through the bathroom window and we all became good friends for many years.

The Northwood Rec gave way, in the early '60s, to another Saturday night record hop. This dance was in a church hall and didn't smell. We also could wear shoes in this one, except after the rare floor waxings, which was good.

By the time of this hop, called the Northwood Appold Dance, we had the core of our gang in place. Most of us would enter through the front door, some through the rear windows. I guess that was out of habit because, as far as I remember, the dance was free.

Once inside, we'd leave our coats and jackets in the coatroom by the entrance and then walk down a short flight of stairs to the hall.

In those days, the girls and guys were always kept separated unless dancing. The boys lined one side of the hall, the girls hugged the other. That arrangement was fine with us. Most of the guys in our crowd were shy and probably would have ignored the girls even if they stood right beside them. The other thing was that we were quite the mischief-makers back then. I doubt many of the girls would have stood still for our shenanigans.

I regret saying that most of the guys I knew smoked back then. At this dance, once you were inside you stayed in. If you went outside for any reason, during the course of the evening, the door would lock behind you. Therefore, we would take our smoke breaks in the men's room.

On one ocassion, during the first Northwood Appold dance, an elderly woman named Miss Tilly, who had been given the unenviable task of controlling us, walked by the hallway men's room. She noticed smoke billowing out from under the door and assumed the place was on fire. Upon opening the door to investigate, at least a dozen teenagers stampeded out while others screamed in embarrassment.

On other subsequent evenings, sink spigots disappeared in the on position. Sink drains would be clogged with hand towels, causing a flood. Toilet paper rolls constantly found their way into toilet bowls. Off-color messages, written in soap, would appear regularly on the men's room mirrors.

Such was the burden poor Miss Tilly, and her helpers, had to bear.

At the end of the evening, we would all assemble for what was called the fellowship circle. In the circle we joined hands around the elderly volunteers for prayer and reflection. At least that was the original intent of the ritual. It eventually became a way for Miss Tilly to call out and acknowledge suspected culprits and then verbally humiliate them for their sinful ways.

At one dance, during the winter, a few of us left a couple of minutes early (probably to avoid the fellowship circle). We were putting on our coats in the coatroom when we noticed the different styles and fashions on display there. We began sorting through the apparel and trying on coats until we found one we liked. Then we'd exchange it for the one we wore to the dance.

The members of our group, who were not at the dance, were so impressed by our selection that they went to the hop the following week just to get a better coat.

This became a regular thing after a while. Everybody ended up doing it. Every week a bunch of guys would leave a few minutes before the dance's official closing and head for the coat room. Invariably, as fate would have it, you ended up, at some point before winter's end, with your original coat. What goes around comes around (I think that was a fellowship circle quote).

We did enjoy the record hops and dances. For a while, it seemed like every church and recreation hall was having them, and most of the time we did behave and even, on rare occasions, danced.

TURKISH TAFFY AND OTHER DELIGHTS

When I was a kid, the best thing about candy was that it was cheap. There was even a small country store a few short miles away where they still sold penny candy. Most of the candies that I bought were the candy bars, and they sold for a dime. The most expensive candy bar then was The Chunky, a small square mound of chocolate, raisins, and nuts that sold for a whopping twenty-five cents.

Some of my favorites from those times are still around today. They include Milky Ways, Twizzlers, Raisinets, and Whoppers (malted milk balls).

My two favorite candy treats from those days have, unfortunately, gone the way of the dinosaur.

One is the Milkshake bar. It was sort of a poor man's Milky Way when eaten warm, but put that bar in the freezer for a while, and then eat it, and you had a chocolaty piece of heaven.

The freezer worked wonders on some candy back then, but you had to be careful. Put the wrong bar in a freezer and you would have an uneatable mess that wouldn't even taste the same when thawed. A Milky Way was another good example of freezable candy. But, I can tell you from experience, you did not want to freeze Snickers, Three Musketeers, Butterfingers, or Baby Ruths.

The best-frozen candy, and my favorite candy of all time, was the Bonomo's Turkish Taffy bar. The taffy came in four flavors, Natural Strawberry, Natural Banana, Natural Vanilla, and Natural Chocolate. I liked them all but the chocolate, and would frequently alternate between the other three. I guess that if you pinned me down and forced me to give you a favorite flavor, it would be vanilla.

It was tempting to eat them straight from the shelf, and they were certainly good that way. But if you had the patience and fortitude to stick that same bar in your freezer then wait a half hour, you'd have the candy the way it was meant to be eaten.

When it came out of the freezer, you would need to snap it. Snapping it meant grabbing an end of the thin bar and slapping it against the kitchen counter. You would snap it enough to break it into small chunks. If it crumbled a little, you probably overdid it, but still no problem. You could slide those small slivers into your mouth at the end.

I once saw a friend of mine take a hammer to his frozen bar. This was a bad decision, as he witnessed when he opened the wrapper to find only slivers. The rule of thumb of any freezable candy was to never break them apart by any artificial means, including kitchen utensils and items found in your father's toolbox. If the treat could not be broken by hand, it was not meant to be frozen.

Anyhow, it's refreshing to still see most of those candy bars still on the shelves today. Just be careful what you freeze, okay?

LIFE IN THE ALLEYS

One of the things I was most thankful for while growing up in Baltimore city were the alleys at the rear and side of my row home. In the 1960s, alleys were pretty much used for everything except parking. I don't remember ever seeing parked cars in our alleys.

In the late fifties and most of the sixties, vendors would use the alleys to hawk their wares. I cannot tell you how many Saturday mornings I was rudely awakened to the sound of horseshoes on asphalt accompanied by a voice yelling "TOPSOIL!" as loudly as humanly possible.

The horse and cart vendors would usually appear on Weekend mornings selling either topsoil or vegetables. I could understand vegetables, but I could never quite figure out why anyone would spend money on dirt. We certainly had plenty of it in our neighborhood. Maybe I was just upset at being woken up by dirt salesman.

The good vendors would start showing up around dinnertime. The Good Humor man (who, by the way, always seemed angry), was usually the first to arrive. Then came the snowball truck followed by the Mister Softee Truck. For some reason, I always felt bad for the guy driving that truck (their cherry sundaes were great though).

With the exception of the surly Good Humor man, the vendors weren't always regular. So if, for example, you decided to pass on the fudgesicle, toasted almond bar, strawberry shortcake bar, or popsicle, you were taking your chances.

I spent many a summer evening waiting in silence for the soothing Mister Softee loudspeaker chords of 'Old MacDonald Had a Farm' that never came.

The alleys served another purpose for the kids in our neighborhood. They were makeshift playgrounds. All you needed on a summer day, to start up a game of handball, was three or more kids, an alley, and a pinkie.

As I said earlier, no one ever complained when, at least fifteen or twenty times a game, the pinkie ended up in someone's yard. We would just hop the fence and retrieve it. Adults were a lot more tolerant back then of kids running around in their gardens.

We'd even play hopscotch in those alleys, using chalk to draw the board, and the rubber heel off one of my father's shoes.

On cold winter nights, we would splash buckets of water down our alley's slight incline and allow it to freeze over. The resulting ice slide provided hours of breakneck fun. As good-natured as the neighborhood adults were, I do seem to remember that the ice flows, usually located in the vicinity of where the residents put out the morning trash, caused ill tempers.

Whenever we walked to any friend's house in those days, we always used the alleys for the commute. We used back doors much more frequently than the front.

Alleys are still around today, but are not the multi-functional playgrounds they once were. A couple of years ago, I revisited the alley on my childhood block and was shocked to see many cars parked along its sides. What a waste of good handball space.

SEWER PIPE EXPLORING

Of all the stupid things we did as kids under the guise of adventure, sewer pipe exploration was undoubtedly the most idiotic.

Looking back on it, I can only think that at some point we must have ran out of intelligent ways to amuse ourselves to stoop so low (if you'll pardon the pun) as to crawl through sewer pipes.

It started innocently enough. During one of our expeditions through our neighborhood woods, we came across a sewer pipe drain. It was under a old bridge that crossed the stream that split the woods. The round opening was about three feet above the stream and maybe four feet high. A trickle of brackish water flowed from the concrete tube.

There were five of us in the woods that summer day; myself, my brother, and three of our friends. After staring into the dark void for several minutes, it was decided that two of us would venture into the hole while the other three waited at the opening listening for screams.

I, along with a friend named Mike, volunteered to check it out. We were given a couple of packs of matches, and, I believe, our last rites, then sent on our way.

Due to the confined space, we had scuttle crablike through the pipe, bent low at the waist and crouching. For a time the brightness of the opening provided enough light to see. After a while however, the pipe curved into darkness and we needed to rely on matches.

We realized rather quickly that the match as light idea was ill conceived. They provided little illumination and only lasted a few seconds before burning a couple of fingers. And, as if that weren't bad enough, in the blackness, between match lightings, we would hear scurrying sounds and other weird noises.

At some point, after we had shuffled for some distance, Mike made an unfortunate reference to a movie we had just seen called *The Time Machine*. In that movie, an ugly race of humanoids named the Morlocks lived below ground and used sewer pipes, similar to the one we were in, to get around.

I became certain that those hairy hunchbacked Morlocks were now all around us, kept at bay by the tiny flickering flame of our shrinking match supply.

We decided to head back to the entrance as quickly as possible. As we got closer to daylight and freedom, we began to smell something funny. The odor was of something burning.

As we crawled nearing to the opening, the smell became more intense. Then we began to see wispy smoke in the gloom when we lit a match.

We found out later that our friends left behind found themselves bored waiting for our return. They decided to use the matches they had left to start a fire.

It was our misfortune that they started the fire at the entrance of the sewer pipe. As I said earlier, nobody ever accused our gang of being intelligent.

When Mike and I realized that our exit was blocked, and with the smoke becoming thicker, we had no choice but to turn around and shuffle back into the darkness.

With our match supply dwindling, we traveled a good distance in the dark, using our hands to guide us. The smoke had driven all thoughts of Morlocks out of our heads. We simply wanted to survive to see the sun again.

We had traveled what seemed like a mile when suddenly we saw tiny streams of light from above us. The smoke was now quite a distance behind us, but an acrid burning smell still hung in the air.

The light came from a manhole cover several feet above us. A rusty iron ladder set in the concrete tube led up to it. Mike and I climbed the ladder. I led the way, and when we reached the top, using all the strength we could muster, we pushed the heavy cover to the side.

We found ourselves in an alley of a neighborhood we didn't recognize. Some kids, who were playing nearby, saw us emerge, dirty and soot covered, from the depths and were frightened enough to run away screaming.

We had made it. We survived the smoke, the darkness, and maybe even the Morlocks. We replaced the cover then tried to get our bearings. Mike and I discovered that we were in a community several blocks from where we began.

We hiked back to the woods, sore, smoky, and pissed-off. As we neared our departure point, we noticed that the guys had not only extinguished the fire, but were in fact in a relative state of panic, thinking that they might have accidentally killed us.

They were much relieved (and a bit shocked) when we came upon them from the opposite direction. Some angry words were spoken and I'm pretty sure that Mike threw a punch at one of them. But before too long, all was forgiven and we resumed our trek along the stream bed.

THE PATIO

Hanging out in the decade of the '60s was much more of a challenge than it is today. We didn't have malls in our part of town back then. I imagine they were scarce everywhere. Unlike the teenagers of today who swarm into the comfort of enclosed shopping areas to congregate, we had to make do with outdoor facilities as meeting places.

The store proprietors of our youth would utilize any means at their disposal, up to and including fire extinguishers, to clear us out of their establishments. Today's mall security forces seem to have surrendered to their numbers, leaving the teens to run rampant in the aisles. Not that we wouldn't have done the same thing if we could. But truthfully, even if it meant staying warm, we weren't thrilled hanging around in the Hecht Company bargain basement or Epstein's clothing bins.

Our gang preferred to hang out in the evenings and weekends in front of an elementary school a couple blocks from my house. The school had three entrances. The side entrance facing a wooded area was enclosed on three sides, which was nice, but it also smelled of urine, which was not. The second entrance, facing a side street, would have been a great hangout except it was already spoken for by a bigger gang with a mean disposition. Therefore, by default, we took the front entrance to the school.

It turned out to be a great choice. Even though a two-lane highway was a mere block away, there was a refreshing sense of privacy about the place.

We called it the patio, because it looked like one. When my brother and I couldn't get hold of any of our friends, we would simply walk to the patio and wait. Before long, someone would always show up.

After a while, the word got out that it was a great meeting place. Teenagers from all around would travel to the patio on summer days and nights to congregate. It became a launching pad for many adventures at any time of the year.

On the patio, we didn't have to worry about shopping center security officers or irate store managers wielding fire extinguishers. Back then the patio offered the best scenario a hangout could provide; to be left alone.

Eventually, later in the decade, when the armed forces, college, full-time jobs, and marriage beckoned, the patio fell silent and reverted back to its original intent. But I'll bet the ghosts of our past still haunt the place, talking about baseball, football, comics, movies, record hops, and girls, mostly girls.

RIDING IN THE TRUNK

During our teenage years in Northwood, there was only one thing more important than securing beer for the weekend, and that was finding transportation for those same Friday and Saturday nights.

It was considered a coup to score both. It happened, just not that often.

The Northwooders were not choosy when it came to beer. In fact, any beverage with alcohol content was lavished with attention. That was not the case with cars. We lived by the adage 'the bigger the better' when it came to our automobiles. If you couldn't fit three in the front, and four in the back, it was useless to us. Our reasoning was simple enough. Usually there were no more than five of us dateless on any given weekend night. That left two spaces in the car for members of the opposite sex. Quite often those spaces went unoccupied. Occasionally however, trolling the neighborhoods would produce a girl or two willing to sit between two sweaty guys for the bribe of a cheeseburger and a coke from the local drive-in.

There were times, though rare, when a group of three or more girls would be hungry enough to accept a ride. If the surplus girls were not willing to sit on a lap, and most preferred not to, we would simply drop off a guy or two on the curb. Whoever was driving the car had that option. If you owed the driver money, or had recently engaged in an argument with him, you were probably going to be walking.

Sometimes the unlucky Northwooders would realize they were miles from home and opt to ride in the trunk. Take it from me, this was not an easy decision.

Opting for the trunk was a humbling experience especially while cute girls were looking on and snickering. One teenager in the trunk could commiserate with the spare tire while reflecting on the evening's scarce virtues. Two in the trunk was the ultimate test of friendship. Occasionally first time *trunkers* would realize, much to the dismay of the vehicle's other occupants, that they were claustrophobic. The resulting yells and screams would quickly frighten both male and female passengers alike and severely dampen the aspects of a romantic evening for those with the freedom to move about..

If you were not claustrophobic, or not smart enough to fake it, you might find that getting into a vehicle's trunk was much easier than escaping it. On rare occasions, the purr of the engine and the total darkness might lull a *trunker* to sleep and, with the absence of screams or other activity, the driver and the vehicle's occupants would simply forget you were there.

Often a sleepy *trunker* would find to their dismay that, upon awakening at four in the morning on a city side street, a '57 Ford's trunk was not only sturdy but also relatively soundproof. As a result, those sleeping comfortably in their row home bedrooms would fail to hear the frenzied kicking or cries for assistance. At that point, it often became the responsibility of an observant milkman to implement the rescue operation, or, if your already bad luck took a turn for the worse, the driver's father would hear you on his way to the car for work.

A car trunk was also an easy way to sneak your friends into the local drive-in movie theater. A large trunk could snugly hold as many as four teenagers for a total savings of two dollars for the Saturday night double feature.

Trunk riders were chosen at random, but the rule of thumb was always *no one in the trunk who had recently enjoyed a meal of burritos or any variation of Campbell's Pork and Beans.*

I had a hand in implementing this rule when, as we were pulling up to the drive-in theater's cashier one Saturday evening, one of my two trunk buddies developed a severe case of indigestion. Those long agonizing minutes between the drive up line and reaching the rear of the parking area were the longest of my teenage life. When the trunk was finally opened, the outside air, even with its odor of stale popcorn, was the sweetest I'd ever smelled.

The drive-in incident effectively ended my participation as a *trunker*. These days I'll gladly open my car's trunk for groceries, luggage, and other large items, but I sometimes find myself holding my breath as I do so.

THE MELLO-MEN

The Northwooders eventually reached the age where we enjoyed cracking open a beer or two or sipping on a glass of wine on a weekend night. Unfortunately, for us that age was around sixteen and you had to be twenty-one to buy alcohol in Maryland.

Left to our own devices, we did the best we could to obtain alcohol. Usually those methods involved porching or bribery. We were not above patrolling outside a liquor store in hopes of finding a sympathetic or greedy adult to add our stash to his purchase. Sometimes that strategy worked but most often the adult was more greedy than kindhearted and he pocketed our money.

The beer of preference was of the malt liquor variety. Not because of its taste, but because it contained more alcohol. It packed a stronger punch. The two popular brands were Colt 45 and Country Club. Country Club was the more popular of the two. It came in a small ten-ounce can, and was tolerable warm. A beers taste at room temperature or above was important to us because, during the warmer months, that's the only way we drank it.

If the beer was found or purchased on a summer weeknight, it spent at least a day or two in the warm Northwood woods waiting for the weekend. When it was finally consumed, if we remembered its hiding place that is, the brew was the outside temperature at best.

Sometimes, if the containers were exposed to the sun, they would be hot and angry enough to hiss by just being picked up. Smart drinkers would know to open those beers as close to the mouth as they could. Young men of an impatient and naive nature would often watch in sorrow as the foamy nectar geysered onto their shirt and the ground below.

Wine was a suitable alternative when beer was not to be found. Our gang knew not to be choosy when it came to wine choices. Our creed was plain and simple. If it was cheap we'd drink it. More often than not, we'd be drawn to the sweetness of Bali-Hai, but usually we would end up with either an inexpensive Port or Muscatel.

Speaking of beer not being found. In our group, it was a common occurrence to simply forget where the stuff was hidden a few days before. I can remember many Saturday evenings in Northwood when we would trek to where we thought our liquor was stashed only to find it not there. Invariably, at these times, a frantic search ensued, with several Northwooders scouring the brush and rocks at the woods edge in frantic search for their booze. A few weekend nights were spent drowning our sorrows with ammonia cokes when our searching proved fruitless. Usually, due to the sheer volume of spirits hidden, we'd be successful. It was always a thrill to discover a six-pack of beer thought lost from the previous summer, or to find the unopened bottle of Muscatel forgotten from a long ago porching excursion.

During the winter months, me and my brother, and most of our gang attended the Saturday night dances at the Northwood Appold Recreation Center. The center was a short four-block walk from the woods. That made it convenient in the sense that we could meet and socialize before hand among the moonlit trees. The beer and wine, if found, would be well chilled by the elements. The conversation would usually evolve around the girls that might be in attendance. Any boasts made during this time involving dancing, or even possibly making out, were made cautiously. The past had proven that, even under the influence of malt liquor, we were an awkward group when it came to the opposite sex.

Usually the dances took place on the basement level of the center. A long table held the record player, speakers, and stacks of 45-rpm records. The records were bought a couple times a month by the Fellowship Committee, which consisted of two to four women. The number varied on a weekly basis. Dropouts among the Fellowship Committee were not uncommon. The guys who attended the weekly dances were, for lack of a better word, rowdy. As I stated earlier, practical jokes and immature pranks took place on a regular basis at these dances. Though not mean-spirited by nature, they took their toll on any adult with a sense of dignity and decorum.

Miss Tilly (of the smoking men's room and the fellowship circle) was the one committee member who would not be intimidated by our pranks. Miss Tilly was older than the other women, and was able to tolerate the weekly shenanigans with no apparent psychological damage. Though she could be gruff and a bit surly at times, Miss Tilly was the glue that held those dances together.

At each dance, Miss Tilly would try her best to get the boys on one wall to socialize with the girls on the other wall. Occasionally Miss Tilly would drag a boy and girl to the center of the dance floor and force them to dance hoping it would kick-start a chain reaction. That rarely worked however. The most successful method was the 'ladies choice' dances. The boys who were hand picked to dance rarely had a choice. No girl was going to walk back across that dance floor without a guy in tow. To assure that fact, the young women crossed the floor in groups of three and four. They had enforcers with them.

On the rare Saturday evenings when a group was secured to perform, the dances were moved to the upper level where a stage and tables were available. These first floor dances were highly anticipated affairs because they featured local groups performing high-energy foot stomping rock and roll. To our gang, who spent many a Saturday night listening to the likes of Bobby Vinton and Paul & Paula, the live dances were pure heaven. They were so well liked that the Northwooders made certain that, on the night of the event, the woods was stocked with as much liquor as we could porch or purchase.

On one such Saturday evening, the Northwooders gathered in the woods an hour before the dance. We had been told the previous week that a 'special' live group would be performing that night. The rumor during the week had been that a well-known artist or group would be appearing. Chuck Berry's name came up, as did Del Shannon, The Drifters, Duane Eddy, The Ventures, and Little Richard. Someone even mentioned Doug Clarke and the Hot Nuts as the featured guest, then Miss Tilly's name was brought up and that line of thought quickly evaporated.

The two six packs and a wine of a questionable vintage (the label was missing) porched during the week were quickly consumed and we hurriedly made tracks to the dance.

When we arrived at the scene, the crowd gathered in front of the center confirmed what we already suspected. An event of legendary proportions was to take place this night. Due to the upper level dress code, the males present wore ties and sport coats. The girls, who wore dresses to all the dances, looked pretty much the same. Greetings were exchanged with friends from adjoining communities. Cigarettes, which were forbidden inside, were hastily smoked just in case the men's room was well guarded. Eventually, after one final dress-code inspection, we made our way into the packed facility.

Round tables and folding metal chairs adorned the walls on either side of the stage. There was a rather large open area directly in front of the stage reserved for dancing, and plenty of room for socializing on the floor between the tables. The stage itself was curtained off. Even amid the din of the assembled masses, we could hear instruments, in that hidden space, being tuned and tested. Our friend Ben, who was feeling the effects of three Country Clubs with a wine chaser, loudly proclaimed that, based on his instrument tuning knowledge, the group behind the curtain had to have been The Beach Boys.

This pronouncement soon spread throughout the auditorium, sending boys and girls alike into a state of frenzy. Requests for *Surfin' U.S.A.* and *Little Deuce Coupe* were directed at the curtain. Some guy even asked for *In My Room* before he was stared down. Things were beginning to get chaotic, with arguments over songs and lyrics, when Miss Tilly took the stage.

Immediately the crowd quieted. By the time she stood, in front of the curtain, at mid-stage, you could have heard a pin drop.

"Young men and women," she began. "I know many of you have waited patiently for this night to arrive and I promise that you will soon be rewarded. But first I would like to announce some important events on the fellowship calendar."

Someone said "Oh crap" loud enough for her to hear it, but she ignored the remark.

From her pocket, Miss Tilly produced a long piece of paper and began to read. Several endless minutes later, her committee duties done, she cleared her throat. "And now, without further ado, it is my honor and privilege to welcome our special guest group of the evening. Ladies and gentlemen, all the way from York, Pennsylvania, I present to you The Mello-Men."

There was a stunned silence as the curtain opened. On the stage were thirteen young musicians dressed in white tuxedos. Most were sitting behind stands that appeared stolen from the Lawrence Welk Show. To the rear of the stage stood a matronly looking woman, whom I assumed was their chaperone since she lacked an instrument and wasn't a man.

The hushed silence of the crowd did not seem to bother The Mello-Men in the least. They promptly broke into their first song of the night, 'Love Letters in the Sand'. As there were no microphones on stage, this number, as well as all their remaining selections, was an instrumental. That fact did not seem to bother several girls in attendance, who grabbed their dazed boyfriends and dragged them onto the dance floor.

Our gang simply stared at the stage thinking that maybe this was a hallucination brought on by the wine with no name. That line of thinking quickly evaporated when the Perry Como medley was announced.

73

At somewhere around the ten-minute mark of the medley, Ben, who was distressed that the music was in his words "causing him to lose his high", began to look for a way to express his displeasure. He decided to heave an empty coke bottle at the stage.

For some reason, known only to him, he intensely disliked the third sax player on the left. He approached the stage and took careful aim at the young Mello-Man. Just as his arm cocked back, Miss Tilly, seemingly appearing out of nowhere, snatched the bottle from his hand and spun him around to face her. Ben, now more sober than inebriated, had enough of his wits about him to tell Miss Tilly that he had lost his balance and had outstretched his arm to prevent his fall. So proud was Ben of this lie that he actually thanked her for keeping him upright. For her part, Miss Tilly gave Ben the benefit of the doubt and let it slide, under the stipulation that he drink no more coke for the remainder of the evening.

And so the night went on. After awhile, the music became less annoying as we socialized with the guys and even some of the girls. The Mello-Men's *tribute to big bands* later in the evening did move most of us into the unguarded men's room, where we enjoyed a smoke and some quiet reflection.

By ten o'clock, The Mello-Men ended the dance much the same way they started it, with a Pat Boone song, *April Love*. There was a smattering of applause from the girl's side of the floor, but not a single call for an encore, when the curtain came down. The rush to the Titanic's lifeboats surely could not have been more frantic then the stampede through the dancehall doors once they were unlocked.

Unlike other Saturday nights, no one loitered around outside the center to reflect on the evening's virtues. Ben perhaps said it best when he remarked that he needed to get home and *wash out his ears.*

The Northwood Appold dances went on through March of that year, 1963. There were no more first floor dances during that time. We spent the remaining Saturday nights in the customary confines of the basement. After The Mello-Men, complaints over Bobby Vinton and Paul and Paula dropped off significantly. The girls still had to wait for a 'ladies choice' song to dance. The men's room still filled with smoke. And Miss Tilly still bore the brunt of our pranks with determination and grit.

1963 marked the end of the dances at Northwood Appold. The era of sock hops, and recreation hall dances, was, for all intents and purposes, coming to an end. The Northwooders moved on, as we always did, to other endeavors, both mischievous and heartfelt. And the Mello-Men dance took its rightful place in the history of a young Northwood.

THE TIMONIUM DRIVE-IN

Drive-in movies were distinctly different from their fast food counterparts in this regard. You didn't go to drive-in movies to pick up members of the opposite sex. You had better have one in the car with you. Because, as any teenager back then knew, the drive-in was the one place you could park with your boyfriend or girlfriend and not have to worry about a cop's flashlight shining in your window.

Unlike today's vehicles, which separate the driver and passenger with a console, the standard sized cars then had smooth vinyl seating straight across the front of the car. It was like having a sofa behind the steering wheel.

You always wanted to remember to bring a blanket for privacy, but that was about it. The drive-in provided the food and the entertainment.

The first thing one did after paying the small admission fee (it was around fifty cents a person) was to secure a good parking spot. Usually it was in the middle or the back of the lot. Secondly, one needed to check the working condition of your speaker. They were the heavy clunky boxes that would attach to your driver's side window.

In the Timonium Drive-In, in Baltimore County, at least fifty percent of them were either missing or not working. Not that many of my friends cared, but I thought the movie dialog made good background noise to the mischief going on around it.

And while we're on the subject, I'm ashamed to admit that on at least one occasion I became interested in the movie playing at the time. The movie was *Nevada Smith*. Even today, watching that movie on DVD, I can only enjoy it by glancing at it out of the corner of my eye.

Our local drive-in always played at least two movies and sometimes as many as five or six if you wanted to make a night of it. During the break between the features the viewer would be pummeled with some of the tackiest commercials ever created, urging you to try the concession stand's food and drink. They also had a big clock occupying a corner of the screen. The clock would tell you how much time you had before the next feature. I think that when it got down to two minutes, it would turn red and pulsate.

Let me say this right now. In my opinion, our local drive-in had some of the worst food ever served by man. Even the mess hall grub I had to endure a few years later in boot camp was better. The popcorn seemed stale by weeks. The hot dogs were green and would break in two if bent. The egg rolls were hard enough to be weapons, and the sodas were diluted and under carbonated. Yet come intermission, everyone would flock to the concession stand.

Speaking of intermission, one particular commercial still comes to mind after all these years. No, it was not the talking hot dogs or the coke and Pepsi cups engaged in a sword fight. This particular commercial featured an idiotic kid who wanted a popcorn mine.

A genie somehow appeared in front of the ten-year-old imbecile and told the boy he would grant him a wish. Did this kid want a million bucks? No! Did this kid want world peace? No! What this goofy youngster wanted was a popcorn mine. That's right. When faced with the prospect of wealth and prosperity, this kid chose an abandoned mine filled with popcorn.

Well, he got his wish; an old mine stuffed to the rafters with popcorn.

I imagine him today, middle aged, poor, and bloated from years of popcorn abuse, wondering why he made such an unwise choice.

THE 1964 NORTHWOOD SCHOOL FAIR

By the summer of 1964 I had stretched out my adolescence to the breaking point. The following summer would find me working in a warehouse in downtown Baltimore. The summer after that, boot camp in Fort Gordon, Georgia. The next summer, Long Binh, Vietnam.

Many events and adventures with the Northwooders were yet to come, but the summer of '64 was my farewell to the enchantment of the season, before work and responsibility pushed the magic of those days aside. Thankfully, it was a great summer, maybe the best of my younger years. It began, as every summer did, with the Northwood School Fair.

The Northwood School fair was the event that marked the official beginning of summer vacation. Our school semester ended the third week in June. The school fair was always the last Saturday of that month. The contingency plan was to have it the first Saturday in July if there was a rainout, but, to my recollection, that never happened. The Saturday of the fair was always a beautiful early summer day.

The fair was held mostly outside (the candy and plant sales were indoors) at the rear of the school.

I guess you could say it was sort of a combination flea market/amusement park. Tables were set up around the school's perimeter for selling contributed items like clothes, tools, and even records. There were also stands selling hot dogs, sodas, snowballs, and cotton candy. The fair also had pony rides and various beanbag-tossing games.

The festivities began at nine am, but my brother and I would get there early to help a friend's mom set up the tables. After that, we were on our own. Our pals would start showing up one or two at a time during the morning hours until all were present and accounted for.

Let me say right now that it was never our intent to create mischief at the fair. We always started the day in a courteous and polite fashion. But on this particular afternoon, after checking out all the tables, playing most of the games, and eating a couple dozen twenty five cent hot dogs, we became restless. Sitting on the crest of a grassy hill, watching all the action, some of us noticed a child open a rear door to the school before being scolded by his mother.

The Northwooders happened to know that rear door was always locked because we had often tried to enter it on weekends. We simultaneously looked at each other with the same thought in our heads; a hangout.

We raced down the incline and into the door and found ourselves on the first floor of a stairwell. For a while, we were content to lounge around on the steps, listening to the commotion outside. Before long, we became restless, tired of sitting and talking, and decided to explore a bit.

We discovered another door at the top of the steps. It too was unlocked and we were pleasantly surprised to find it opened up into the school gym.

We couldn't believe our luck. What started out started out as a somewhat forgettable stairwell adventure had now suddenly developed into much more. The gym had ropes hanging from the ceiling and tied down to the walls. An assortment of balls littered the floor from small dodge balls to huge medicine balls. A large piano occupied one corner of the facility.

I'm not sure to this day the purpose of a piano in a gym. It was an elementary school, so maybe the kids climbed ropes to the music of Beethoven or Mozart. At the time nobody paid it much mind. The ropes held most of our attention.

Once they were untied, we began to swing around the room with wild abandon. It was such a unique thrill to have a fully functional gymnasium to ourselves that we sent an envoy outside to spread the word.

Soon the gym was filled with dozens of young men taking advantage of this once in a lifetime opportunity All the ropes were being used by at least one boy. Some had two or three hanging from them. Balls of all sizes flew about the gym, some aimed at the swingers, others at the walls and ceiling.

At some point, it was decided that the piano would make a good launching pad for the ropes. We rolled it to the center of the gym and while one talented young man played a medley of Jerry Lee Lewis standards, we jumped off its surface, swinging out on our improvised Tarzan swings.

It was around this time that we realized our shouts, yells, and the off-key rendition of Great Balls Of Fire had drawn the attention of a few adults. We saw them crowded outside the door that led to a school hallway. Fortunately for us, that door was locked from the inside.

The adults were desperate in their attempts to access the gym. From the door's small glass opening we could see their mouths moving frantically, but the din in the room prevented us from hearing their words. One woman in particular seemed in obvious distress. Every time a guy would mount the piano she would open her mouth wide in what looked like a scream, but, as I said, we couldn't hear her.

Suddenly it appeared that a light bulb turned on simultaneously over all their heads. They had figured out our point of entry.

As fun as this was, no one really wanted our day to end with police officers escorting us home.

We took off in a flash, at least thirty of us, leaping down the stairwell and out the door. Adults outside scattered to avoid being trampled by the onslaught. It was several seconds of sheer chaos.

Most of the guys mixed into the crowd, heavy panting the only obvious sign of their shenanigans. Our gang headed back up the hill in time to see several quite angry adults enter our former hangout.

The remainder of the day was a rather normal affair. A couple of us were kicked out of the plant room after a shoving match knocked over some azaleas. One of our gang took a pony ride when he thought we weren't looking. But we saw him and gave him grief throughout the summer. But mostly we ate hot dogs and cotton candy and talked about how we'd spend the rest of our vacation.

I can't remember how many more years the Northwood School Fair continued. It wasn't many. It was, despite our occasional ill behavior, a unique social event that defined the innocence of the sixties. Like many memories from that time, it was irreplaceable.

Oh, by the way, that door was tested many times during the course of the summer, but we always found it tightly locked.

SCHOOL'S OUT FOR SUMMER

I can't vouch for my friends, but for me the last day of school before summer vacation was a magical time.

The day dragged on. There is no denying it. The final hour before the last bell of the school year rang was quite possibly the longest hour of all time. By now, most of the teachers had given up too. There was no studying or verbal interaction. Everybody, the students, the teachers, the principal, the custodial workers, and the truant officer, stared silently at the clock.

When three o'clock finally arrived, and the loud clanging bell sounded for the final time that year, we all jumped out of our chairs and ran for the doors.

Anything left behind, books, papers, pens, articles of clothing, stayed there.

It was really a wonder that no one was killed or maimed in the ensuing rush to fresh air.

I remember the last day at my junior high school. When the three o'clock bell rang, I joined the mad exodus of bodies pushing toward the front door. I was ten feet from the door, from freedom, when I slipped and fell.

I really thought it was the end. I could see the green grass and trees. I could smell the clean summer air, even with all the sweaty kids around me.

Then, suddenly, strong arms grabbed me and lifted me up. It was my mechanical drawing class teacher who, caught up in the excitement of the moment, was leaving the building also, even though he was required to stay until later in the afternoon. I nodded my thanks and shot out the door.

As I ran into the warm June sun, I resisted the temptation to look back. My buddies up ahead were yelling for me to hurry. The summer was a young and impatient friend. Its wild adventures wouldn't wait forever. I had lost precious time when I fell.

I ran faster to catch up with them, and, when we joined together, I did turn around for one final look.

The school was far enough in the distance that it seemed small and harmless. I can't remember for certain, but I probably smiled and maybe even laughed a little. I had made it. I was safe.

It had been a small victory, one I would certainly forget in time, but it was the moment I knew that the summer had won.

MUSIC, RECORD PLAYERS, AND LOOSE CHANGE

I grew up on rock and roll, as did most of my generation, but my earliest recollections were not of Chuck Berry but of Broadway.

My parents (I think it was more my mother) enjoyed Broadway musicals. They had just bought an enormous piece of furniture that was part television set, part record player, part radio, part storage facility, and topped off with large speakers. The unit was so big and cumbersome that if one had the misfortune of dropping something behind it, it stayed there. The thing was just too heavy to lift and try to move. I still don't know how anyone managed to get it in our house to begin with. I was at school when it was delivered and only returned home to see the last ambulance pull away.

I was not allowed to play my 45s on the thing. My mother used the record player exclusively for her collection of show tunes and Victory at Sea albums.

My earliest 45s were a standard collection of popular rock and roll of the time, by artists such as Ricky Nelson, Del Shannon, Buddy Holly, and Gene Pitney.

Most of my 45s were purchased after watching the weekly top twenty countdowns on the local favorite dance show, The Buddy Deane Show. It is worth mentioning that some of the more popular Buddy Deane songs did just so-so nationwide. But if they hit his chart, I bought them.

I remember having a tiny record player that I used exclusively for playing 45s. My player got a lot of use on a daily basis. If I liked a song, I would play it repeatedly. I rarely had the cash or the inclination to purchase phonograph needles on a regular basis. Therefore, when a 45 started to skip from wear and tear, I would simply weight down the phonograph player's arm with coinage.

I would usually start by taping a penny or dime to the flat surface above the needle, then work my way up the monetary system. Eventually, on particularly skip-prone 45s, I'd have close to a dollars worth of change on the player's arm. At that point, quite frankly, the needle became a lathe. You could almost see the tiny slivers of vinyl peeling off the record's surface.

I recollect, at one time, admiring my future wife's impressive record collection. She had records by artists and groups that I had somehow missed in my collecting.

After we married and I delved in to her stack of platters, I was dismayed to find that they were too worn to be listenable. I guess the two dimes, one nickel, and a quarter secured to her record player's arm should have been a giveaway.

At some point, around the time of the British invasion, I started to buy albums. Albums were good because you had a nice fifteen-minute break between flipping them to the other side. They were also harder for parents to toss in the trash without your knowledge, due to their size.

In that long ago era, music provided the backdrop for almost all our activities. Transistor radios, record players, and jukeboxes filled the air with rock and roll. No matter where you were on any given day, if you stood perfectly still, and listened as hard as you could, you would hear music. That was the joy of rock and roll. It did not need to be loud to bring a smile. Just the thought of it would usually do the trick.

GOING TO THE MOVIES

In the sixties, going to the movies meant two things. Either you were lucky enough to have a date and went to an evening show, or (if you were too young to date or just an unfortunate soul) you went to a matinee with your buddies.

If you were fortunate enough to have a movie theater close by, matinees in the late fifties and early sixties were pretty cool. The theaters near our neighborhood showed almost exclusively horror movies in the afternoons (which in that time meant monsters) or sometimes science fiction movies (monsters and robots). Occasionally one not associated with that genre would show up, like West Side Story (more about that one later), but more often than not you went to matinees to be scared.

One any given Saturday, or weekday during the summer, our gang would decide to take a break from the heat or the rain and see a movie. Sometimes as many as twenty of us would hit the theater. Once we paid our quarter or fifty cents (at some point there was a price increase) to get in, and after we rummaged through the concession stand for snacks, we'd grab our seats, usually five or six rows from the screen.

Once the theater darkened and the featured movie came on the screen, there was a respectful minute of silence before noise erupted in the theater. Unlike today's movies where the occasional cell phone ring tones break the silence, back then, it was all out war. Yells and screams pierced the air. Foods and liquids rained down on all the patrons. Critiques and suggestions were often shouted at the screen.

I sometimes wondered about the adults who brought their children to the shows. I can't recall them ever saying a word. They simply sat there and took their punishment in a silent and dignified manner.

Some of the lousy movies I saw at matinees were The Giant Claw, The Horror of Party Beach, The Monster That Conquered the World (actually it didn't get out of the San Francisco Bay harbor), Eegah, The Magnetic Monster, and I Was a Teenage Werewolf, to name a few.

Some of the better matinees were The Thing, Them, The Incredible Shrinking Man, Godzilla, Rodan, Forbidden Planet, The Creature From the Black Lagoon, The Time Machine, Curse of the Werewolf (and all the other Hammer horror films), and War of the Worlds.

But the best matinee all of all time and the one that I sat through (along with most of my friends) at least eight times in the summer of 1962 was West Side Story.

I don't know what it was about that movie that made it the perfect matinee fare, but it was. Our gang and many other guys in our neighborhood flocked to see it.

Watching it now on DVD, it comes across as kind of a chick flick, what with the guys dancing and singing and the love lost ending. But then, in the darkened Northwood Theater, we found nothing wrong with the singing, dancing, or the ending. I suspect our reason for liking it was a combination of things. The music, though not rock and roll, was hummable and good to whistle to on the walk home. The story held our interest although I can tell you right now that our gang was never in a rumble, didn't carry switchblades, and didn't pick fights with cops. Quite the opposite. If any of us sensed the bad vibes that proceeded the meeting of fists with flesh, we'd get the heck out of there. We liked to think that we were lovers not fighters, though we weren't much in the way of lovers either.

I believe the main reason we continued to come back to West Side Story was Natalie Wood. Though none of us would admit it, I believe we all had a crush on Natalie. She was just so damn cute in that movie. I think we felt that if someone that looked like Richard Beymer could get her, that maybe we too had a shot.

I recall a first date with a girl named Mary Lou who lived on the same street as my mother. On a warm summer night, we walked the ten city blocks from my mother's house to the Northwood Theater. I believe I was fifteen at the time.

When we arrived at the theater, I realized that I had forgotten my wallet. Fortunately, Mary Lou had enough cash in her purse to pay for our way in. She also was kind enough to pay for my milk duds and soda.

I had every intention of paying Mary Lou back, but I didn't see much of her after that. I do remember her brother telling me several months later that for some time she required her dates to produce their wallets and be able to state the exact amount of money they had on their person.

I took my future wife on our first date to see The Bridge on the River Kwai. It was at a theater three miles away. I didn't have a car so we walked both ways.

This time I remembered my wallet. My wife confessed to me, after we were engaged, that the long walk almost ended our budding romance. I imagine a missing wallet would have finished it off.

GETTING AROUND WITHOUT A CAR

I didn't get my first car until a couple of months before my wife and I were married in June of 1968. It was an MGBGT (a hardtop MG), a neat little two seat sports car. We were living in New Jersey at the time. I was still in the army, stationed at Fort Monmouth.

The sports car seemed like a good idea at the time, but I eventually came to the realization that it wasn't a practical choice. This realization struck me somewhere between exit ten and twelve on the New Jersey Turnpike. It hit home when I looked over at one of the many trucks passing me and noticed that its wheel was taller than my car. I was driving along at seventy miles an hour in a car where my butt was about a foot off the asphalt. My legs stretched out under the car's engine and I was not wearing a seatbelt (nobody did back then). In reality, my car was a coffin on wheels.

On top of that, I was usually driving back to Baltimore after working a twelve-hour shift. I would usually find myself dozing off near the vicinity of the Delaware Memorial Bridge and waking up on the Baltimore beltway. I still don't know to this day how I made it home some of those nights.

I often try to think if it was my future wife's father who talked me into purchasing that little car. We didn't see eye to eye on most things. In particular, he didn't think I should be dating his daughter, and I thought I should. He was big and Italian (I swore he was in the mafia) and never smiled, save for the time I told him I was going to Vietnam, then a large grin split his face.

Anyhow, I made it through a couple of years with that car. Turns out it was pretty dependable. It really didn't start acting up until a day or two after the warranty ran out.

Before that, when I was in high school, I had five ways of getting around: borrowing my father's '58 Chevy Wagon, catching a ride with a friend, walking, thumbing a ride, or taking the bus.

I will tell you truthfully that the last three options were worst-case scenarios. Unfortunately, more often than not, I ended up using one of those modes of transportation.

Until my last year in high school, when my brother and I were lucky enough to acquire a friend named Dave who had a Volkswagen Beetle, I was very much at the mercy of the public transportation system or the general public.

I know of grandfathers who would tell their grandchildren tales of walking miles to school in the most horrendous weather conditions. That wasn't me. Oh I walked to and from school, many days (my high school was about two and a half miles away), but only under favorable weather conditions. If the weather was lousy, I'd either thumb or take the bus.

Hitching a ride was easy going to school. I'd simply walk across the street by my house and stick my thumb out. Usually within five minutes, I had a ride. I should add that thumbing a ride in the 1960s was an accepted practice. Many kids did it without incident. In fact, the only incident I'm aware of was when a buddy of mine was touched on the leg by an older male driver. My friend told me that he proceeded to punch the guy in the head, then jumped out of the still moving vehicle. My pal was all right, and he never ran into that man again.

Hitching a ride from school was harder because of the competition. On most of the traffic lights surrounding the school you'd find as many as twenty guys angling for a ride. If someone pulled over, at one of those lights, it was much like the paparazzi and a movie star. The vehicle would be swarmed with bodies all grabbing for the door handle, or even the hood or the trunk.

I would often walk a block or two up the road to a less congested intersection. Or sometimes, after walking those two blocks, I'd just say the hell with it and keep walking.

The worst part about walking home was carrying all those books. We didn't have backpacks then. Some kids had them, but they would get beat up for it. Backpacks, or book bags, were, for a reason I can't explain, taboo at our school. Therefore, if one liked an unbruised face, they would keep their notebook, and classroom books under their arm. The only saving grace we had was a large rubber strap with hooks on each end. The strap secured the books together until it either stretched out until it was about six feet long or wore out and snapped at an always inappropriate time.

For me, the public bus was the last resort for two reasons. The first reason was that it was always packed with kids. Where all the kids came from I'll never know since our stop was the first in front of the school. The drivers, who I suspect were a little sadistic, would never close the doors on a potential fare. The problem was when you yanked the cord for your stop; you usually couldn't negotiate the crowds to get off.

The bus driver, always impatient, would only wait a few seconds before he shut the doors and took off. I remember once, by the time I exited the bus, I didn't even know where I was. The second reason was that I had usually spent my quarter for the bus on snacks in the cafeteria, thereby leaving me penniless and walking.

Thank God for Dave and his Volkswagen Beetle.

TARZAN SWINGS

Before I begin talking about Tarzan swings, there is something you should know about me and my brother, and most of the guys we hung out with, and that is we were reckless.

I suppose you could substitute the word reckless with stupid and still be correct, but we certainly, if nothing else, lacked good common sense (a trait that still haunts me today).

I could give you many examples of our reckless behavior and I will in the following paragraphs, but I'll start with this one.

My brother Steve and I had a woods not far from our house. It was about a mile long and maybe four blocks across, with a stream that ran though its center. Many interesting and exciting adventures transpired in those woods. This tale will concern three of the many incidents that occurred there. The first incident (and, for that matter, the other two) points out the reckless/stupidity factor.

A four-lane bridge crossed the woods at its center. At its height, it stood about forty feet above the stream below. The bridge's underside had three curved concrete arches. They ran the length of the span on both sides, and were about eighteen inches wide.

Steve and I, and one or two of our mentally challenged friends, would crawl across those arches on our stomachs, inching up through the pigeon poop on the incline, then gripping the cold concrete as we slowly negotiated the downward slope. The entire time, due to the shortness of the surface's width, a few inches of our shoulders, sides, and legs hung off in the air.

When bridge climbing began to lose its appeal, we moved on to other means of idiotic behavior, one of which was swinging through the air on ropes.

It started with us using the vines wrapped around some of the trees in the woods. We found out the hard way that most tree vines were not sturdy enough to support a well-fed, medium sized boy. We would always test them first by giving them a few good yanks, but, invariably, the first vine swinger would find himself in the dirt below, still grasping the tree part.

Many heated discussions would follow these attempts concerning the merits of woods vines versus jungle vines. We came to the conclusion that the jungle vines, used by Tarzan, were of a sturdier, more dependable nature that the ones found in small woods. We decided to ignore the trees, heal our bruised bodies, and try making our own swing.

This brings us to the second event, our homemade Tarzan swing.

In the woods, there were plenty of thick branches from which to secure a rope. Our problem was that we couldn't find a rope. None of our parents had one to spare, and we were too impatient to save up the money to buy one. There was one item, however, that our parents had plenty of, and that was clotheslines.

Since no one had a dryer back then, all our wet clothes were hung outside on clotheslines. I myself found it quite humiliating to have my underwear constantly on display for the entire neighborhood to see. I would sometimes wear my underpants wet just to avoid the embarrassment. Anyhow, a few of us decided a clothesline would do just fine as a rope substitute. So we grabbed an unopened package off my mother's washing machine and headed for the woods.

We found a good sturdy branch overlooking the stream. The tree was climbed and the clothesline wrapped around the limb. After it was tested thoroughly, much like the vine testing, I decided to be the guinea pig for its first launch.

I stood on the hill ten feet above the stream, clothesline secured in both hands. A warm summer breeze buffeted my face. I felt empowered; much like an astronaut must feel shortly before lift-off. I gripped the clothesline hard and, with the encouragement and cheers of the gang behind me, swung out.

I was directly over the stream when the clothesline broke. I fell the ten feet and landed on my right side in the six-inch deep water. I lay there in a daze for a few seconds, not fully comprehending how I came to such a fate. When the reality of the situation (and the cold water) brought me to my senses, I yelled for Steve to go get my dad.

My brother and friends ran off to fulfill my request and soon it was just me amidst the cold running water in the silence of the woods. I lay there for awhile fully expecting my life to flash in front of my eyes at any moment. After a minute or two however, I realized I wasn't really hurt. In fact, besides being pretty wet, I felt fine.

I got up, wrung some water from my shirt and pants, and headed home. I actually made it to the front door as my father was leaving in a panic (it turns out he was in the shower when my brother burst in) . When he saw that I was fine and was, in fact, just a bit wetter than he was, he smiled in relief. It was only later, when he discovered our Tarzan swing had been a clothesline, that he got pissed-off.

The next summer we found the best Tarzan swing of all time. It was also in the woods, but farther up and away from the stream. Someone in our gang heard of it by word of mouth. Several times we looked for it to no avail. The stories about the swing were of mythical proportions. One day we decided it must be found at any cost. When we finally did come across it, we knew the rumors were true. It was the Holy Grail of Tarzan swings.

It was constructed of thick rope high up on the huge limb of a monstrous tree. The daredevil that climbed that tree and out on that limb, to secure the swing, must have been very brave indeed. The rope hung out above a muddy ravine. It was accessed from the starting point on a steep hill overlooking the barren area.

The swing was useable in two ways. One could swing straight out and back in the standard Tarzan swing mode. Or one could (with a running start) swing out in a roundhouse circular fashion and swing around the perimeter of the ravine. That last function is what gave the swing its A+ rating.

It also had a stick knotted at its base. The user could use the stick as a handgrip, sit, or stand on it. That was the beauty of the swing. It was multi-functional.

At the far edge of the ravine, and directly across from the swing's launching point, sat a tree stump. It was not high enough to impede one's swing. It was however, a good place to stand if one wanted to hitch a ride on the swing at its apex. I must say at this juncture, that every boy who attempted to join his companion on the swing (myself included) at its halfway point failed miserably. Usually the attempt would result in a collision that would cause both to fall in the mud. Sometimes just the stump guy would fall and the swinger would be left twisting in space several feet above the ground. At other times, the stump jumper would simply misjudge his leap and fall butt first into several inches of mud.

It just never worked, yet every time we used the swing someone would stand on that stump waiting to be humiliated.

The novelty of that swing never wore off. On any given summer day, you would find as many as twenty boys gathered around the ravine waiting their turn on the ride.

At some time, over the course of the harsh winters, the rope became too rotted to use. None of the Northwooders wanted a swing bad enough to climb out on that high limb and attach a new one.

We moved on to other equally reckless endeavors, but as the years passed, that swing became the stuff of legends. Often, when my brother and I, and old friends, get together, we talk of its awesome wonder.

THE BEST CHRISTMAS

I don't know about you, but for me Christmas was the best day of the year (the last day of school before summer vacation comes in a close second).

Christmas morning was always great fun for my brother Steve and me. I stopped believing in Santa Claus when I was seven or eight years old, but I still believed in getting presents no matter who or what the source.

My parents were happy to oblige us. They were always generous in their gift giving, and never failed to keep us busy, in the early hours of December 25th, opening presents.

I don't mind saying that nowadays, though still exciting, Christmas is a lot less the event it was back then. These Christmas mornings my wife and I usually sleep in then enjoy a cup of coffee before opening up our gifts.

There happens to be one Christmas I remember quite fondly. My parents lacked adequate storage areas in our row home. This particular holiday my brother and I received a couple of larger items, a pool table and a couple of bikes. One morning, about five days before Christmas, we saw that there was a sign on the basement door. It read 'KEEP OUT'. Because our basement door did not lock, keeping us out of there would have probably required an armed guard. About thirty seconds after reading the note, we snuck down there and were overjoyed with what we saw.

Of course on Christmas morning we acted surprised as hell when we tore down the basement steps and once again laid eyes on our goodies.

One quick note about the pool table. It was not one of the fancier models. In fact, it was somewhat cheap. We had to keep putting stuff under the legs to keep it level (eventually it became about a foot higher then when purchased). Then to top it off, the surface beneath the felt was some type of plywood, which didn't hesitate to warp in our humid basement. After a while, Steve and I became rather adept at playing on the crooked thing and supplemented our allowances playing against friends unfamiliar with plywood surfaced pool tables.

Warps and all, my brother and I loved that pool table, and, once they were able to conquer the tricks of its stubbornly uneven surface, our friends did too.

GIRLFRIENDS

In Late 1963 or early '64, my brother Steve began dating a girl named Carol. This would normally have not been a significant event. A few of our gang were dating back then. What made it special was that Carol had a sister and between them they had friends, all girls.

Up until that point, our gang never really hung out with members of the opposite sex. I guess that, by today's standards, we were late bloomers. It's just that there was always more fun to be had hanging out with the guys than going out on a date.

A good example of this was the time when one of our friends was coerced into taking his date to see 'My Fair Lady'. Then after the movie, to add insult to injury, he was made to sing the entire lyrics to *The Rain in Spain* before his date would let him get to first base.

The next day, when we gleefully related to him our adventures of the night before with the guys, our friend angrily swore off girls until the year's end.

As it turned out, Carol's house was a hangout of sorts for her and her sister's female pals. After school, they would meet there for a bit before homework and dinner.

My brother was able to persuade the sisters to allow our gang to occasionally meet there in the afternoons, under the condition that we not go near the refrigerator or any breakable objects. Of course, we agreed. It was the winter after all, and too cold to gather outdoors.

The house eventually became a great after-school hangout. The girls were attractive, fun, and nice (in fact, I ended up marrying one of them), and it was a short four blocks from my home on Burnwood Road.

After a while, our good behavior (we didn't break anything and only raided the fridge on rare occasions) allowed us to go there on weekend evenings.

Carol's parents, as it turned out, went out often on Friday and Saturday evenings. The girls would inform us of their absence by the following method. If the front porch light was on, the parents were home, if the porch light was off, they were out.

Many a chilly weekend night was spent in the wooded area across from their row home waiting for that porch light to go off. Sometimes the parent's car was gone but the light stayed on. We surmised that on those times, the girls just didn't feel like dealing with us. Fortunately, most of the time the light went off on cue and we'd run out of the woods cold and grateful.

Unfortunately, it was on those nights when stuff did get broken. We'd play games like 'hide and go seek' with the lights off (as I said in other pages, these were innocent times), and sometimes, in the dark, things got a little rowdy. The sisters always had a good excuse for their parents who I'm certain, after a while, thought them to be either extremely clumsy or very poor liars.

Later on, when some of us began to date, we used the basement for make-out sessions. Because of privacy issues, only one couple were allowed in the basement at any given time (we were banned from the second floor bedrooms for the obvious reasons). So we implemented a kitchen timer to monitor each couples basement stay. On crowded nights, it was fifteen minutes per basement visit. On less crowded evenings, it would go up to thirty minutes.

We did have some flexibility with this system. When the timer went off after fifteen minutes, the basement dwellers had the option of evacuating the area or buying a part, or all, of the next couple's time. If you were lucky enough to follow a particularly horny couple, there was good money to be made. Some of our gang who were broke, purposely followed these couples just to make a buck. But most of the time the kitchen timer rule worked like a charm.

The girls became known by our gang as *The Rat Pack*. I'm not sure how that label started but it seemed appropriate at the time. I think the girls just called us *The Idiots*. But they did, for the most part, tolerate our antics and we ended up participating in many adventures together.

The guys and girls still did things together even after I enlisted in the army.

When I returned from Vietnam, I proposed to one of *The Rat Pack* members, Veronica. We married six months later.

And yes, after almost forty years together, we still occasionally set the timer for fifteen minutes and head down to our basement.

SUMMER VACATIONS

We were fortunate as kids to have relatives who lived on a farm. The farm was located in Troy, Ohio, which was about an eight-hour car drive from our house. I'm still not sure what their relation was to our family. I believe they were like third or fourth cousins. All I remember is they always seemed a bit surprised when my father's car pulled up to their farmhouse. I kind of think my father forgot on occasion to tell them we were coming. At least once, I remember my dad bringing some type of official document from the courthouse with him to show them that we were indeed related.

The last time we went there was in 1960. I was thirteen and my brother was eleven. We brought a friend along with us for that final trip. For us urbanites, going to the farm was like visiting an alien landscape. They had cows there, a bull, some sheep, and lots of chickens. Besides the farmhouse, a full-fledged barn with tractors, tools, and a hayloft graced the property.

The barn would always be our first destination upon our arrival. While my father, stepmother, and our older cousins were examining the court documents we would run to the barn. Once there, we'd play around on the tractor, find hiding places in the hayloft, and look for bats and toads.

They had many acres of property. Cornfields covered a good bit of it. The cornstalks were always high and

107

abundant during those summer days, and we would spend hours during the day wandering through the maze of cornrows trying to get lost, and sometimes succeeding.

Dinner was always our favorite time of day at the farm because the food was always so fresh. Fresh food was a genuine treat for boys who normally subsisted on leftovers. The vegetables were always picked fresh in the morning and, though I never witnessed it, I imagine the chicken was too.

My brother, our friend Ben, and I even enjoyed getting up at the crack of dawn to feed the animals and gather up chicken eggs.

We would normally spend about a week on the farm before going back to the land of asphalt and concrete, but each of us loved what little time we had there. It cleansed us, recharged us, and gave us great stories to tell our friends and classmates.

My father also liked to camp and, for two or three years in the early '60s, would take my brother and I with him on camping trips.

The trips would only last two or three days, but they would always be thrill packed. I saw my first eagle on a camping trip. It flew directly over our car on a small dirt road. For an instant, its shadow blotted out the sun. Then it was ahead of us, flying slowly, the tips of its wings nearly touching the trees on either side of the road.

I also saw my first bear that was not caged. It was at night. My father, my brother, and I were talking around the small campfire over the babbling of a stream a short distance away. We suddenly heard loud splashing from the water nearby. My father concentrated his flashlight beam on the running water. It illuminated a bear in the water, a big one, holding a fish in its huge paw, staring back at us.

My father calmly, and without saying a word, turned off the flashlight, got up, strolled into his tent and zippered it all the way up. I guess he forgot about my brother and I. Left to fend for ourselves, we followed his lead and swiftly entered and zipped up our tent.

We huddled up in our dark surroundings waiting to hear the rustling of the hungry giant predator lurking about in our campsite. At some point, my brother alarmed me by quietly announcing that he heard the growling of the bear nearby. Thankfully it was just my father snoring in the other tent. I guess the bear did not bother him as much as it did us.

One time, my father and I went exploring in a wooded area in Pennsylvania known as New Germany. After trekking for a while, we realized we were hopelessly lost.

I remember that we climbed a tall hill, hoping to get our bearings. As we neared the hill's crest, we began to smell something peculiar, like rotten garbage.

When we reached the top, we saw the reason for the odor. We were on the far side of an expansive landfill.

We eventually were able to hitch a ride to our campsite in the back of an empty garbage truck. Despite the smell, riding in the rear of that garbage truck with my father was the highlight of that summer.

COLLECTING STUFF

Ah, the joys of collecting stuff. It's an obsession I never outgrew. I collected stuff in the sixties, and I'm still collecting stuff today. Just ask my wife who can hardly step foot in the basement without having a panic attack. Today, it's mostly stuff I'm planning to sell. In those days I had no intention of ever letting go of my collectables.

In my youth I collected stamps, match pack covers, coins, comic books, records (45s and albums), baseball cards, trading cards, and most any type of reptile I could get my hands on.

I won't spend much time talking about coins and stamps. They were boring things to collect, and I'm not sure why I bothered. I guess it seemed like a good idea at the time.

A few years ago, I ran across a small book of mint stamps from my youth. Thinking I might have the opportunity to make a few bucks, I called some dealers. To my dismay I found out that they not only didn't increase in value, some had actually decreased in their net worth.

I found it rather odd that the five or ten cent stamp of yesteryear would only be worth three cents today. Apparently, they are worth more stuck to an envelope than in a stamp collection. My mother was bewildered last Christmas when she received her card in an envelope with nine five cent stamps on its cover.

Match Pack Covers

I had tons of these and I didn't even smoke. They were easy to collect because they were all over the place. It seemed like everybody past the age of sixteen smoked cigarettes back then. If the packs still had matches in them, they were no good. They had to be match free. That was no problem. If you looked at the ground while walking a few blocks in any direction, you would retrieve dozens of them (littering was much more acceptable back then). There was a great variety of designs and pictures on those covers, and I'd be willing to bet they're worth more today than stamps are.

Comic Books and Famous Monsters

I have always enjoyed reading, and there wasn't anything better than a comic book on a hot summer day. They were cheap (a dime a pop), easy to read, and quickly forgotten about when it was time for a pick-up baseball game. My favorites early on were *Dennis the Menace*, All the DC superheroes, particularly *Superboy*, *Superman*, and *Batman*. I also liked *Blackhawk* comics, also on DC. Later on I got interested in Marvel comics. Marvel had some great superheroes including *Spiderman*, *The Fantastic Four*, and *Thor*, and I had a mess of them. But the Marvels I remember most fondly were the monster comics that came out a couple of years earlier. They were issued under the banners of *Tales of Suspense*, *Amazing Adventures*, *Journey Into Mystery*, *Strange Tales*, *Tales to Astonish*, and *Amazing Adult Fantasy*. They had some great monsters with names like Monsteroso, Sserpo,

111

Gruto, Manoo (it seemed like these monsters liked their names to end in O), and Gargantus (Garganto must have been taken).

Speaking of monsters, I'd be remiss if I didn't mention the best magazine of all time: *Famous Monsters of Filmland*. *Famous Monsters* magazines weren't issued with the regularity of comics. They came out every three months or so. Finding them in a drugstore was a hit or miss proposition. They were so sought after by impatient young men that if your timing was off, the store would sell out and you'd miss an issue.

My father looked out for me in that regard. He would always check the newsstands and magazine racks when he made his cigarette purchases. I had a feeling that he was also looking for the current issue of *Stag* or *Adam*, but I didn't care as long as a *Famous Monsters* fell into my hands.

In 1961, at the age of fourteen, I made the acquaintance of a large tree while sleigh riding in the Northwood woods. Early in on my five-day stay in the hospital, my father brought me three issues of *Famous Monsters*. One was current and two were back issues that I'd missed. I never asked where or how he found them. Those three magazines, with their werewolves, mad scientists, and lizards the size of tall buildings, took me from the bleakness around me to a world where the fantastic was as real on the pages as it was on the screen. It was possibly the best gift my father ever gave me.

About five minutes after I left for boot camp in the summer of 1966, my stepmother tossed my comics, magazines, and anything else that had a front and back cover and pages in between, in the trash. I guess I should have hidden them better. *The Fantastic Four* comics alone would have probably subsidized my retirement.

Records

On Saturday mornings in the late fifties and early sixties, I never missed a local dance show called *The Buddy Deane Show*. Saturday mornings would feature the top twenty record countdown for the previous week. I would sit in front of the T.V., pencil in hand, watching as Buddy went up the list from twenty to one. If a song appeared on that list that I didn't have, I'd beg my father to get it for me.

Later that day, after I wore him down, my dad would drive me to the Radio Music Center on Greenmount Avenue in Baltimore. They simply had the best selection of 45s around. Once there, the owner, who went by the name of Froggy, would supply me with my musical fix.

In those days, it was all about 45s for me. I could have cared less about albums. Those times would come later. My goal for those short few years was to have the complete *Buddy Deane Show* top twenty each week and, thanks to the patience and the wallet of my father, I succeeded.

Later on in the decade, 45s took a back seat to LPs, but I still picked up the occasional 45 right up into the 1980s.

Baseball and Trading Cards

Any boy (or girl) who collected baseball cards in the late fifties and sixties knows a few things. There was always at least one player card that you needed to complete your collection that was impossible to find because, for one thing, all your buddies were looking for the same player. There were always lots and lots of duplicates. It was not unusual to have many more duplicates than originals. The packs of cards came with a hard, almost unchewable, cardboard like flat piece of gum. I could spend a lot of time just talking about that crappy gum, which was more of a weapon than a food product. One of my pals almost lost an eye when one was errantly thrown his way.

Anyhow, the duplicates were mostly used for pitching. Pitching was simply a few kids throwing baseball cards at a wall and if your card was closest to the wall at the end of each toss, you won the cards. Cards leaning against the wall or leaners, as we called them, were the best. Unfortunately, after a few days of pitching, most of the cards were so bent up and frazzled that they were only good as coasters for our soft drinks.

After a while, I became more interested in trading cards. I liked the graphic *Mars Attacks*, the western *Roundup* cards and my personal favorites, *Davy Crockett* trading cards. At some point, I had the complete sets of each. I really wish I had the foresight to hide them away in a safe dark corner until I gained the knowledge of their eventual worth. Mothers, and for that matter almost everyone else, had no concept of future trading card value. Anything in my room small enough to fit in a trashcan and made of cheap cardboard or paper was just visiting before making a final home in a garbage truck.

My mother, when confronted about missing items, would never admit to the theft. Her memory would fail her at these times. She would not remember seeing the cards, or records, or comics. She would tell me to search my room thoroughly and, while I was at it, straighten the room up a bit.

I am sure that at some time during those frequent search and clean missions, the trash collector would visit the back alley outside my bedroom window. Little did I know that while I was picking up my room, they were picking up my cards, records, and comic books.

ADVENTURES IN THE WOODS

Northwood is a relatively small section of Baltimore city. It is located in the city's northeast corridor about a mile south of the city limits. Northwood, for the most part, was built in the early 1950s. An area now called old, or original, Northwood had been around for several years prior to that.

Though Northwood was part of the city, and featured row homes, it had a suburban feel to it. This was due to the plentiful open areas surrounding the houses. There were several fields and small tree lined parks within walking distance of our home. Eventually houses took over some of them, but a few are still there today.

The best undeveloped area for our gang was the woods. The woods served to divide an older section of Northwood from us, the new kids in town. It was not very wide, maybe a quarter mile at most. It was perhaps around two miles long, though the part we traveled was less than a mile. The stream that ran through its center also varied in width. For most of its length one could wade across it without getting their knees wet.

Though the apex of the woods was quite level, years of erosion had taken a toll on its sides. To gain entry to almost any part of the woods you needed to negotiate a steep incline. The safest way to do this was to scuttle down the steep hill crab-like on your butt. But if you were unfortunate enough to be caught attempting that maneuver, at the very least you were likely to have an unflattering nickname for the remainder of your adolescence.

Therefore, most of us would tackle the hill in a dignified upright position, knowing full well that by the time we reached the bottom we'd be running ungainly, arms flailing, just trying to keep our balance.

Once the woods leveled out, there was much to explore. On the northern side, near the entry point, a swampy area covered the flat ground. We mostly avoided this territory for obvious reasons. Occasionally one of the guys would attempt to navigate the swamp only to get bogged down in its muck. One could easily spot the kid who dared to explore the swamp. His legs would be muddy and quite often he'd be missing a tennis shoe. Most of us were content enough to stay on the trail that led from the incline to the stream.

Once at the stream, the options seemed endless. You could head upstream, where the woods and the stream widened out, or you could venture downstream, where the water ran shallow enough in spots to bathe in, if you wanted to risk a tetanus shot.

The problem with hiking upstream was that before too long the woods came to an abrupt undignified end at a large storm drain. However, if you went downstream, the woods seemed to go on forever. I can't recall ever walking to the end of the woods in that direction. I seem to remember that something about the unfamiliar territory ahead would always spook us into turning back before we got too far.

Sometimes we'd venture into the woods for an hour or two, but usually, during the summer, we'd make a day of it. Lunches were packed. Mothers were given instructions on the distribution of our comic books and baseball cards should tragedy strike. Band-Aids were stuffed into pants pockets, and off we'd go into the warm morning sun.

Exploring the woods never became boring. There were always places to discover and adventures to be had. Sometimes a mass of trees would open to a secluded cove, secretive enough to hide from any imagined predator. Trees yielded vines to climb on. Small foothills, several feet above the stream's sandy embankment, often resulted in spectacular jumping contests.

Sometimes old trails, perhaps made by Indians, were discovered and followed. Often it was just fine to walk the stream. There was always the challenge of finding just the right sequence of rocks to allow you go from one side to the other while staying dry. From time to time we would come across the perfect rock somewhere mid-stream; A rock large and flat enough for all of us to sit on for a spell, and listen to the gurgle of water rushing past us.

The woods also held our fascination at night. Our expeditions after dark were often cut short. Invariably something would happen in those dark pathways among the trees that would scare us to the degree that we would scurry up the hill to the well-lit streets. Sometimes a well told ghost story would do the trick. At other times we'd see things. Small glowing lights dancing around the swamp were regular occurrences after dark and moving shadows lurked everywhere. Nor was it uncommon to hear strange animal like noises. One night we heard a howling sound in the distance that served to quickly send us packing, vowing that we'd never return.

During the cold winter months, the woods rarely drew our attention. Sometimes after a heavy snowfall, we would hike through it, and a couple of the tree-lined hills were used for sledding.

But the woods was first and foremost a summer escape. Like a thoughtful friend, it would always be patient enough to hold its surprises until then.

SODA FOUNTAINS AND AMMONIA COKES

As a teenager, I was fortunate enough to have three pharmacies (or drug stores, as some were called back then) within walking distance of my home. Each pharmacy had much to offer a boy in the late '50s and '60s.

During the lazy days of summer the Northwooders would often walk to a pharmacy for one of the main staples of our lives; comic books, baseball cards, candy, or a snowball.

Back in those days, there wasn't a snowball stand on every corner as there is now. In addition, at least in our neighborhood, snowball vendors did not regularly drive up the alley behind our house like the Good Humor man. Therefore, we had little choice but to walk or ride our bikes to the treats.

Thankfully, the closest pharmacy also had the best snowballs. It was a place called The Alameda Pharmacy. It was the hub of the smaller half of a shopping center divided by a road. The soda fountain took up the back left hand side of the store. The pharmacy's fountain had round green cushioned plastic revolving stools surrounding it. The stools had no armrests or backs and would get notoriously slick from perspiration and spilled drinks. Quite often, one of our gang would simply slide off of one and land embarrassingly butt first on the tile floor. Spinning on one, on a hot summer afternoon, was suicidal. The pharmacy also had a few booths for the less daring patrons.

Snowballs didn't cost much, I think they were a quarter, and it was a good thing because they were served in a funnel shaped cup. What a gyp that was! The farther you went down in the cup, the smaller it got. By the time you got to all juice, there was maybe a thimble full left, and that was if you were lucky. More often than not, much like a Dixie cup, the thin waxy paper would often unravel and its contents would leak out of the bottom. This often occurring predicament forced us to bend our necks back and hold the leaky container over our open mouths until all the juice drained out.

On top of that, the snowballs were top-heavy and had to be balanced with delicate precision. One false move and the entire upper ice shelve would be on the pavement. It was such a problem that the women behind the counter would ask that we crush down the treats with our plastic spoons outside the premises lest the soda fountain area look like the aftermath of an iceberg explosion.

For some strange reason, my favorite flavors back then were lemon and spearmint. A couple of years ago I tried a spearmint flavored snowball and almost gagged on it.

We would also walk to another pharmacy a little farther away called The Medical Center. The soda fountain there was not as large, but, man, did they serve a wicked vanilla malted milk shake.

Whenever I went there, which was probably at least twice a week during the summer, I'd order the milk shake. Unlike the snowballs, I always felt I got my money's worth out of the Medical Center's milk shakes.

They cost a bit more than the snowballs, but they would come to the counter in a large aluminum container. Depending on who your server was, you could get as much as two full glasses out of it.

The gang and I also liked Coca-Cola but, when ordered at the soda fountain, the cokes had to be flavored. In those days, you had three basic choices, vanilla, cherry, and chocolate. I wasn't that fond of chocolate flavored cokes, so I would usually alternate between vanilla and cherry. Do not let anybody tell you that those flavored cokes tasted the same as the store bought brands of today. They didn't. They had a much stronger syrupy flavor. Man, were they good.

As much as I hate to do it, I have to bring up another flavor our gang would order...ammonia. That's right; we would drink ammonia flavored cokes. Do not ask me why. I certainly don't know why I drank them and I'm sure my friends didn't either. I suspect we thought that anything tasting that bad would give you a quick high. Maybe we heard it somewhere. Well anyhow, it was an awful concoction that first cleared your sinuses and later your digestive track. The weird thing is we continued to order them in lieu of tastier concoctions much to the amusement of the counter workers.

There is a possibility we might have ordered food on occasion from the soda fountains that we frequented, but, if so, the meal was too unmemorable to recall. I only remember the snowballs, the malted milkshakes, and the flavored cokes.

I guess I should have kept the ammonia coke information from my wife. Now, whenever she's cleaning with Lysol, she always asks if I would like a sip or two first before she starts.

HOME LIFE

Home life in the 1960s was significantly different then it is now in this regard. If you were a boy and over the age of fourteen, you could pretty much go where you wanted without being questioned, with school nights being the notable exception. Don't get me wrong, some parents were strict as hell. It's just that most weren't.

I believe my father and stepmother enjoyed the peace and quiet when me and my brother Steve weren't around. They put up little resistance if we told them we were going out for a while. My father rarely asked where we going. He would simply dismiss us with the wave of a hand, and then resume watching television.

My stepmother, on the other hand, would ask for our destination, but would usually lose interest around mid-explanation and wander away.

Let me say this right off the bat. We never ever stayed inside after school, and definitely not on weekends, or during summer vacation. No matter what the weather, cold days or hot, rain, sleet, or snow, blizzards, hurricanes, earthquakes, whatever, we were out in the elements.

Most mothers didn't work in those days, and no adolescent wanted to hang around the house until a household chore came your way or, worse yet, you were made you open your school books and do homework.

As an aside, I practiced this same philosophy later, in the army. If you had free time, get the hell out of the barracks.

On rare occasions, my brother and I committed the ultimate taboo of spending the night out. We would tell our stepmother that we were staying at a friend's house, while our friend would tell his parents the same thing. Ultimately, we would end up outside on a warm summer evening (we didn't use this scam when it was cold) with the entire night ahead of us.

As I said earlier, those were innocent days. The few times we spent the night out, we weren't bothered by a soul. We'd wander around the community empowered by the knowledge that we were outdoors long after we should have been. We'd go to the elementary school playground and play on the monkey bars (I should note that all the school playgrounds had a concrete or asphalt surface back then). Sometimes we would hike to the shopping centers just to see them devoid of life.

Usually at around two in the morning, the novelty would wear off and we would start looking for a place to sleep. Once we slept in the grass by the school. On another night we snuck into my home's basement to sleep on the floor. It was usually around this time that we wondered why we were sleeping on the ground or a damp cold floor and not my warm comfortable bed. Nonetheless, a month or so later we'd do the same thing again. Such was our insatiable desire for adventure.

There was one time in the day when we would go home. It was when we were hungry. My stepmother wasn't much of a cook, but there always something on the table at dinner time. Those were the days when the family sat around the table and talked or just kind of sat there staring at each other.

On the evenings when hot dogs or sandwiches, were served, we would be allowed to set up a wobbly food tray and watch the black and white television in our dining room. But those meals was rare. Usually our house was as quiet as a tomb at dinnertime.

Lunches, on non-school days, were rarely eaten at home. It was just too risky returning to a parent who might have forgotten earlier in the day that the grass needed mowing.

On most summer days we'd pack a lunch and brown bag it to the woods or the ball field just to avoid going home and unnecessary risks.

Our family lived in a three-bedroom end of row house. My father and stepmother had the master bedroom. My younger brother Steve had somehow finagled his way into the second largest bedroom with a side and rear window. I had the smallest bedroom with one window facing the back alley. I still believe to this day that my bedroom was originally the walk-in closet for my brother's room.

The windows in our house stayed open on summer nights. The exception being my father's room. He had a window air conditioner. My brother and I each had a room fan. He had a large stand up model. Mine was small enough to fit on the nightstand (are you noticing a pattern here?).

Most of the row homes in our neighborhood, and in most communities, lacked air conditioning. We all just made the best of the summer heat. Fans did the trick most of the time. When they didn't, you suffered (and sweated) in silence.

It is crazy to think that there were many nights when we kept the back door open and unlocked, letting a screen door draw in the air. Our neighbors did it also, and I never once heard of anyone being burglarized.

The normal behavior in those days of old may seem insanely foolish now, but it worked for us then, children and parents alike. It wasn't a case of not knowing any better. Our community of Northwood was simply a safe place to live.

AN OBSESSION WITH SNAKES

I loved collecting snakes when I was young. My obsession with snakes began at the age of twelve and lasted until I turned fifteen, the age I began to seriously date girls. At that age, it didn't take me long to realize I had a choice to make. I could either continue hoarding snakes or I could continue dating girls. There were no other options.

I found out within the first couple of weeks of dating that bringing up the topic of my snake collection would effectively end the night's date. In fact, references to reptiles of any sort usually put a damper on things.

I'll give you an example. When I admitted to my wife, a few years after we had married, that I once collected snakes, she sincerely told me we would not have married had she known this while we dated. That's how much most girls hated snakes.

Anyhow, it was a fun hobby while it lasted.

One of the cool things about owning snakes was scaring my stepmother's friends with one of the several in my collection.

My stepmother would invite the same group of friends over our house every month for cards, and every month, without fail, I would walk in on them with a snake wrapped around my neck. Even though they must have known it was coming, they would still scream in panic and try to jump out of the dining room windows.

Eventually the group decided to meet at a house that was snake-free, but it was fun while it lasted.

At one point, much to the chagrin of my father and stepmother, I had as many as ten snakes in my room with me. I had all kinds; corn snakes, Florida king snakes, hog nosed snakes, garter snakes to name a few. Back then, they would ship them straight to your house from Florida. Of course the more common ones I caught.

Despite my best efforts to contain them, from time to time a snake would escape its confines for the freedom of roaming my house. One in particular, a large black rat snake, became the Houdini of the bunch. Despite my best efforts, the five foot snake broke out of the aquarium enclosure at least once a month.

When this happened, I did my best to keep it a secret. My father barely tolerated my hobby, but my stepmother looked for any excuse to rid the house of the things. I'm sure finding one beneath her feet would have been the final straw.

Luckily, I always found the snake. Usually it was hiding somewhere close by. It did manage one final escape however. It made a break for it the night before I gave away my collection. Somehow it must have gotten wind of my scheme.

I could not find the snake the next day, nor in the days afterward. It had simply disappeared into the night, never to return.

Of course I kept this news from everyone else in the house and they never knew of the newest addition to our family for the remainder of the time we lived there.

One summer day, while I still collected snakes, my father took me and my brother to a place outside of

Baltimore called the Rocks State Park. There, while my father fished in the large stream that ran through the park, my brother Steve and I scouted for turtles and tadpoles.

At some point, Steve, who was a bit farther downstream, began to shout loudly. I ran to see what caused the commotion, and saw the tail end of a water snake slither under a rock in the stream about three feet from the shore. Being reckless (and, yes, a little dumb), I reached my hand under the rock and grabbed a slithering coil.

When I raised myself up, I saw that I had the snake by its tail. I held my arm straight out. The water snake was almost as long as I was; its head touched the ground. As I watched, it drew up. Its head traversed up its body until it got to my wrist where the thing proceeded to bite me.

My father had witnessed all this and was now running toward me shouting for me to drop the snake. It didn't take much encouragement. Once the thing bit me, I dropped it like a hot potato, and then watched it calmly slither back into the water.

I noticed my dad had his knife out. He suspected that I'd been bitten by a cotton mouthed water moccasin, which were, and still are, quite poisonous. Luckily, I avoided the knife by displaying teeth marks on my wrist as opposed to the two fang marks a moccasin would have left.

The incident taught me a lesson. From that day forth I always made absolutely sure that a snake was non-poisonous before I grabbed it.

SKATEBOARDING IN THE SIXTIES

My neighbor's teenage son is an avid skateboarder. On just about every afternoon, he's in front of his house doing assorted jumps and tricks that involve the curb and an elevated bar he places in the street. On any given summer day, the sound of wood impacting on concrete will fill the air. His entire skateboarding activity occurs in front of his house.

I certainly wish I had the patent for whatever wood is used for the skateboards of today. My neighbor's board takes severe punishment daily but never seems worse for wear. His curb is an unsightly mess of cracks and missing chunks of concrete, but his skateboard still looks brand new.

A few years ago, skateboard parks were the rage. There were two of them a short distance from my house. But, for whatever reason, they have seemed to have fallen out of favor with the young men of today who prefer curbs to ramps.

In the mid sixties, when the Northwooders were skateboarding, we ignored the curbs in front of our homes. Usually a car was parked there anyway. Truthfully, our skateboards were not made for jumps and tricks. Jumping on one of our skateboards would likely result in breaking it in two, and the only trick we attempted was trying to avoid moving vehicles.

I guess you could say we were the pioneers of skateboarding. Maybe if you lived in California you could buy one, but not in Baltimore. Even if they were on the market, I doubt anyone in our gang would have put out the cash for one, not when you could improvise and make one for nothing. Here's how it worked.

You would get a 2" by 4" board and saw it down to about 18" in length. Then you'd find a pair of roller skates (actually, you only needed one skate). Before I go any further, let me say that the skates back then were not like the skates of today.

In the sixties, the metal skates were adjustable and attached to your shoe. This was done by using a key that tightened front and rear brackets to your foot. Once the skates were attached to your shoes, you were more or less stuck with them until they were loosened. If you misplaced the key, the skates became a permanent part of your shoes. A good friend of mine was forced to throw out a perfectly good pair of scotch grain dress shoes due to key loss.

To complete your skateboard you would take a skate and disassemble it and then nail the two ends on the front and rear of your two by four. Voila, you had a skateboard.

Could you do tricks with it? No. Could you maneuver it? Just barely. Could you go down a hill on it? Yes. And there you had it. Our makeshift boards were good for one thing; going from the top of a hill to the bottom of a hill.

If you tried to get too fancy on one of our boards, a trip to the local hospital emergency room was likely in your future. In fact, just going down a hill was an adventure.

131

We had a few hills in our neighborhood. Unfortunately, they were called streets. No matter what time of day one skateboarded, there was always the threat of a car lurking behind a stop sign, or on a concealed side road.

With this in mind, we usually skateboarded in pairs. One of us would skate while the other practiced traffic control. This was problematic in the sense that the friend (or spotter) on vehicle watch, at the bottom of the hill, would usually be easily distracted. More often than not, a girl or a snowball truck commanded his attention just long enough for his skateboarding buddy to require stitches or a cast.

We did find a loading ramp at the rear of Northwood Shopping Center department store, which provided some safety. The walk to that ramp was a long one, so, more often than not; we took our chances in the nearby traffic.

By the time the well-made, maneuverable boards hit the market, we had moved on to other dangerous activities like Vietnam and marriage. But it was fun while it lasted.

THE CARNIVAL

In Northwood, there were two major events that served to bookend the summer. The first was the Northwood School fair, which occurred the third Saturday in June. The second was the St. Matthews carnival, a weekly event that took place in the evenings from Monday through Saturday, during the third week in August.

If you were to quiz the boys in our neighborhood, one at a time, on the merits of both attractions, the fair would probably come out on top, simply because it transpired in early summer. The carnival, on the other hand came about at a time when depression concerning the upcoming school year was reaching a fever pitch.

The boys of Northwood absolutely hated the summer to end. None of us relished the thought of returning to school. It became so bad that, as the final days of summer neared, grief-counseling sessions were a common sight at our hangout, the patio.

It irritated us somewhat that the girls we occasionally hung around with were, during this time, chomping at the bit to return to classes. There was even a nasty rumor that they even held practice homework sessions to prepare themselves for the school year.

The St. Matthews carnival helped us, in its unique way, to momentarily overlook our impending doom and enjoy what little of our warm weather freedom remained.

The carnival took place on the parking lot on the side of the church. Unlike the moving carnivals that pop up on lots today, this carnival was mostly games of chance. The only real rides they had were a Ferris wheel and merry-go-round. If you wanted to empty your piggy bank of change, then this was the carnival for you.

The carnival offered many booths with spinning wheels of all variety. Some exhibited the usual cheap trinkets, some gave out stuffed animals, and others had plants. There were even a few that doled out booze as a prize. I would like to tell you that there was an age restriction at those particular booths, and there undoubtedly was. But I do seem to recall coming across a fellow teenager from time to time carrying a bottle of Kentucky's finest.

There were also booths that involved tossing a ping-pong ball at something, most often a small bowl of water containing goldfish. If your ball landed in the bowl, you won the contents. Usually it was a goldfish or two, but sometimes it was just a plastic bag filled with water.

Several picnic tables had been set up at the far side of the lot for bingo. This locale was where you would find most of the adults.

My brother Steve relayed to me a humorous carnival story involving the bingo games. It seemed that he and a friend, who had volunteered to check winning bingo cards, conspired to make a few bucks at the carnival's expense. The scheme was simple. Steve's friend would stay close to the table where my brother was seated. After calling a fair amount of letters, Steve would yell out

"BINGO!" at which time his friend would be near enough to check his card. Steve, of course, would not have the correct letters, but it would have made no difference. His friend would verify the winning letters; the pot would go my brother and later, in a concealed area, the booty would be split between them.

Everything was set in motion. The players were in place and the game began.

As luck would have it, my brother actually got the proper letters and numbers and had an official winning bingo card. He excitedly yelled "BINGO". His friend checked and verified the letters and my brother pocketed his winnings. Naturally, his buddy still wanted his half.

Steve tried very hard to get out of the arrangement, but to no avail. The words *a deal is a deal* were uttered many times, and in the end he gave up half of his bounty.

Unlike the Northwood School fair, we were mostly well behaved at the carnival. It was held at a church after all.

It was a nice place to walk around with your girlfriend and impress her with your skill at throwing darts at balloons. Do not let anybody tell you different, there is nothing better than winning your girlfriend a prize at a carnival, except possibly a few spins with the same girl on the Ferris wheel.

And there you had the difference between the fair and the carnival. At the Northwood School Fair, the summer was young and our energy fed off that. The St. Matthews Carnival, that urged the summer to an end, was a more melancholy affair. A time to reflect on days passed. A time to hold the hand of the girl you met in June. The girl who could not wait to go back to school, but for now that was okay too. And if you were lucky enough to steal a kiss at the crest of the Ferris wheel just before it began its downward spin, well, then the summer ended just fine.

SHOPPING CENTERS AND FWENCH FWIES

The three shopping centers that I frequented in the '60s are still up and running today. Their facades have changed to reflect today's environment, but otherwise they look pretty much the same as they did forty some years ago.

The Alameda Shopping center was the closest to my house. My brother and I, and our friends, would walk to the drug store there for snowballs, baseball cards, and comics. They also had a Western Auto car parts store in the shopping center that smelled of new car tires, and boasted a great selection of bicycle accessories. The other retailers in the center, like the A&P grocery store and Epstein's Clothing, were for parents only. We avoided them.

The Medical Center was a little bit farther of a walk, but we'd go there for the pharmacy's malted milk shakes. The shopping center also had a Jimmy Wu's Chinese Carryout. My father would buy chicken chow-mien from Jimmy's a lot, but the Northwooders would go there for their French fries smothered in ketchup.

I don't know how we got hooked on this particular American snack at a Chinese carry out, but we did. The Chinese waiter, behind the counter, absolutely dreaded to see us coming. If he was observant enough to spot us from a distance, he would switch the open sign to closed, lock the door, and hide behind the counter.

He hated to serve us French fries. I'm not sure why, perhaps they had an egg roll quota or something. Sometimes, as we entered the shop, he would simply yell "NO FWENCH FWIE! NO FWENCH FWIE!" at the top of his lungs. But we knew he had them back there, and would simply wait him out until he got tired of us hanging around and threw some in the deep fat fryer.

At a little over a mile, the Northwood Shopping Center had the distinction of being the greatest distance away. It was a full sized shopping center with a Hecht Co. department store at one end and an Eddie's grocery store at the other. A Read's drug store, an Arundel soda fountain, a movie theater, a bar, and a couple of small clothing stores occupied the long strip in between.

The Arundel soda fountain was our main source for the dreaded ammonia cokes that our gang bought with confounding regularity. I'm sure we ordered them because we thought the combination of ammonia and coca cola would get us high. It didn't. For some reason, it just made us pee a lot.

Unlike the fwench fwies man, they women behind the counter loved serving us ammonia cokes (they never ran out of ammonia), and would snicker amongst themselves as they did so.

We didn't really hang out in front of any of the stores. Another group of young men had laid claim to a prime spot in front of Read's and, back then, it was polite not to encroach on someone else's hangout.

If one were to visit those shopping centers today, one would find many different stores on display. Jimmy Wu's, and the fwench fwies man, is long gone, as is The

Arundel with its ammonia cokes. Read's, and the Hecht Co. are gone also, their soda fountains with them.

FIVE AND DIMES

Before there were supersized stores like Wal-Mart and K-Mart, smaller versions existed. They went by the names of Kresge's, McCrory's, Ben Franklin, W.T. Grant, and Woolworth's and were commonly known as five and dimes.

The chain store five and dimes of the '50s and '60s were set up in a similar fashion to today's larger stores. The higher end merchandise would be to the rear of the store, so you'd have to walk down aisles of stuff you really didn't want, but ended up buying anyway.

The Woolworth's and Kresge's in our neighborhood featured basements where the budget items were housed. The budget stuff in a five and dime was real low-end merchandise, or, as my mother used to say, junk. And believe me she would know. My mother was thrifty before it was fashionable in those days, but even she wouldn't venture into Woolworth's basement.

Personally, I liked the basement, and so did my friends. That's where the vinyl records were kept, but it was also where they put the birds, monkeys, fish, and the occasional reptile.

The basement of Woolworth's was a noisy place. You could often hear the commotion from the cages when you walked in the store's main entrance. It must have been a hellish place to work an eight-hour shift, and I guess the employees felt the same way because you could never find anybody down there to wait on you.

The lack of basement employees was fine if you were purchasing a record, but it was a problem if you wanted a monkey. In fact, buying any type of future pet in Woolworth's presented a problem because none of the store workers wanted to handle them. More than once I was given a pair of thick gloves with the instructions "Get it yourself".

Five and dimes had soda fountains also, but my friends and I rarely frequented them. For some strange reason they seemed to attract an older mean-spirited crowd. Soda fountain workers were usually unsociable to us at best, but the elderly five and dime counter workers would be downright nasty to us. I don't know, maybe it was the constant basement noise that upset them.

Honestly, there wasn't much in the five and dimes that cost a dime, and even less costing a nickel. Comics were still a dime there, until most of them went to twelve cents in the early '60s. Packs of baseball cards, and candy bars still went for a dime or less.

Even in the budget basement, the items usually sold for a quarter or so. Of course, the pets were more. You could purchase a parakeet for a mere 5 dollars, and a squirrel monkey could be yours for under forty dollars, but bring gloves, just in case.

Five and dimes never failed to be adventurous places to visit. There was always a thrill of the unknown whenever you entered one. You really never knew what you might find there. Sometimes you were disappointed, but quite often you were not. More than any other stores, five and dimes offered a sense of mystery. They are missed.

141

TADPOLES AND BULLFROGS

In the late 1950s, my brother Steve and I collected tadpoles. Bullfrog tadpoles were easy pickings in those days. It seemed like after heavy rains, almost every good-sized puddle had a tadpole or two in it. We had a particular shallow field, within walking distance of our house, that became an expansive swamp after a summer storm. Steve and I would wait two or three days and then, with tropical fish nets and pails in hand, we would scout the marshy area. The quick and elusive bullfrogs were ignored in favor of their young easy to catch offspring. Usually, after an hour or so, we would have a dozen or so of the tailed amphibians.

Our twenty-gallon aquarium was already prepared in our basement and ready for its new inhabitants. When we arrived home, we hurriedly dropped our catch into their new temporary home.

It took a few short days for the tadpoles to transform into their adult counterparts, but it felt like it occurred overnight. I must admit it was thrilling to observe the metamorphosis. Their tails would shrink as they grew legs and became significantly larger. I imagine it was around this time, as they matured into adulthood, that they realized they were no longer in the large watery swamp of their birth.

Perhaps looking through the aquarium glass at a pool table and washing machine, instead of hopping through reeds and lily pads, did the trick. Or maybe they were temperamental to begin with. Whatever the case, our young bullfrogs quickly developed an attitude and became a noisy bunch, especially at night. It was under the cover of darkness, most often after midnight, that they really cranked up the volume of their croaking. I honestly don't think my parents would have minded some croaking during the daylight hours, but Steve and I discovered that neither was partial to the noise at one in the morning.

The two-floor separation between their bedroom and the basement made absolutely no difference when those frogs started their singing. My bleary-eyed father stated it succinctly early one morning when he said it was like pitching a tent in the Florida everglades. Shortly after his lecture on how some parents had to work for a living and therefore needed a good night's sleep, our bullfrogs found a new home in the Northwood woods swamp.

I'd like to say that our dad's emotional morning plea affected me and Steve to the point of swearing off tadpole collecting. Unfortunately it didn't. The net and pail always seemed to find their way into our hands two or three days after a heavy rain, and not long after that our parents would once again take up residence in the everglades.

THE TALE OF THE SNAPPING TURTLE

A small tree-lined stream ran through our community a few blocks from our house. It ran under a main road, Loch Raven Boulevard, and between the many row homes that dotted our neighborhood. My friend Charlie and I were tossing stones into the stream's clear shallow water one summer morning when one of the big rocks in the center of the stream began to move. For a few brief seconds my friend and I stared open mouthed before we both realized that it wasn't an animated rock but instead a very large turtle.

I didn't hesitate to wade out into the water and chase down the slow moving reptile. I grabbed its tail, proudly lifting my prize out of the water.

It had a snapping turtle in my fist, a big one. The biggest I had ever seen.

I recall that the beast was very heavy and highly agitated. My friend, who was taller and stronger than me, would have made a better carrier. But when he saw the turtle living up to its name, its huge jaws snapping for anything other than air, he begged off.

I lugged the thing home, my pal walking several feet behind me. Every few steps he pleaded with me to return the creature to its home, but I refused. I was sure my heroics in apprehending and securing the turtle would boost my popularity with the guys.

It turned out I was right. Not long after depositing the monster in my backyard, the word of my captured prize quickly spread. Before long, the yard was full of inquisitive boys. I guess I got a little too cocky around this time. I would like to blame what happened next on the adulation being cast my way, but realistically it was stupidity on my part.

I began to tease the snapper by waving my hand and wriggling my fingers in front of its face. The beast either saw me as another food source or was simply angered by my silliness. It drew back on its thick hind legs and, with uncanny speed, leapt up in the air and grabbed my thumb in its massive jaws. Out of fear, I flung it off me before the turtle could get a tight grip. Even so, the thing took my thumbnail as a consolation prize for my finger.

It rolled a couple of times on the grass swallowing my nail in the process. The turtle came to rest in an upright position, quickly got its bearings, and then started at me again, preparing to launch itself for the remainder of my thumb.

By now, all of my buddies had seen enough and jumped the fence. They contented themselves with watching this battle of beast versus boy from the safety of the alley. Not wishing to give the turtle a tastier afternoon snack, I promptly joined them.

The snapping turtle quickly acclimated itself to its new surroundings. It prowled the yard as if it owned it. The thing might have been slow in the water, but in my backyard it was fast as hell. Occasionally it would stop and stare our way, as if daring us to take a step on its newfound turf.

Thankfully, for a while, it occupied itself with the backyard clothesline pole. I believe the turtle thought it

145

was an adversary in its yard domination. For several minutes it engaged the pole in close combat, ramming it continuously with its head and shell as the pole shook and swayed. By the time the snapper tired of its foe, the pole rested at a forty-five degree angle, worn and beaten.

After witnessing that rampage, I was quite content to leave the turtle alone and hope the thing would climb the fence into my neighbor's yard, but when it began to take out its anger, and hunger, on my mother's rose bushes I knew time had come to take drastic action.

I stealthily re-entered the yard while the turtle occupied itself shredding the last rose of a once healthy bush. I again grasped its tail and, holding the fiendish thing as far from my body as humanly possible, ran it back to the stream.

That night I told my mother that a large dog had jumped the backyard fence during the afternoon and devoured her rose bush. She was gratefully thankful when I informed her that my thumbnail was lost protecting her remaining garden shrubbery.

The snapper and I came to a truce of sorts that summer. I stayed away from its home stream, but I did on occasion toss a rose or two from my mother's garden into its watery domain from the safe heights of Loch Raven Boulevard.

THE BAD BATHROOM DAY

In Northwood in the sixties, one never knew what the day might bring. Most days started out normal and stayed that way. Some began strangely then straightened out obediently sometime before noon. Occasionally a day would refuse to cooperate with the laws of science and nature and just remain weird from start to finish. And then there were a few days that began in a normal well-behaved manner before proceeding to spiral out of control, taking the Northwooders along with them. This story concerns one of those days.

My brother Steve and I were young when our parents divorced. It was decided by whoever handled those matters at the time that we would spend weekdays with my father at our original home and weekends with my mother at her new residence. Fortunately, my mother moved close by. A short five blocks away, on the other side of the Northwood woods.

Well, short for Steve and me. Our friends took offense to any walks that didn't end with the purchase of candy or a snowball. To top it off, the Northwood woods separated the two communities. A formidable obstacle to our physically challenged buddies.

When discussing the trek to my mother's house, the guys would always claim that their intentions were good. They would explain to us with sincerity how they would often make it down the hill to the stream in the deep center of the Northwood woods, only to find that the sharp slope on the woods backside would be too strenuous to negotiate. Invariably they'd hang out at the stream for a spell before heading back to more familiar, and less demanding, confines.

When, on occasion, one did make it through, he would often be too exhausted to be much of a companion. Sometimes, on a Saturday morning we would find a buddy curled up on my mother's front porch veranda softly pleading with us to "wake me up when the weekend's over."

Steve and I didn't particularly care. We were meeting another bunch of friends on the far side of the stream. Even though Steve and I were technically part-timers, our new friends welcomed us with open arms. Eventually we joined up to form one large interchangeable group. The guys from our mother's block would hike to the patio on weekdays and our buddies from our father's side would fight the woods on the weekends.

One of the friends on our mother's side was a boy named Hank. It didn't take long for Hank to become an adopted member of the original Northwooders. He was a laid-back kind of guy, so he fit in perfectly with our group. Also, he enjoyed lounging around our hangout, the patio. He didn't even mind our alternative rainy day hangout, the rear patio of the school, which had the unfortunate distinction of constantly smelling of urine.

Because I was the oldest, I was the first in our group to obtain a drivers license. It was not easy getting that license. I learned to drive on my father's 1958 Ford station wagon. The vehicle was huge, as big as some of today's trucks. On top of that, it had no power steering. I considered myself in rather good shape back then, but I remember that, until my arm muscles developed, I would have to stand up to make turns.

The parking portion of the driving test gave me serious problems. Turning the stubborn steering wheel while maneuvering into a small parking space, even using both hands, was a near impossible task. Eventually my test instructor tired of my struggles and he grabbed the wheel too. Between the two of us, we managed to park the damned thing.

Once my arms looked like Popeye's, after eating his spinach, I was fine. It actually became a fun vehicle to drive in spite of its size. I would drive it across all terrain. Hills, wooded areas, baseball fields, parks, and median strips were all challenged in our quest for thrills.

It just so happened that on the bad bathroom day I had possession of my dad's Ford wagon. It was a lazy mid-summer Saturday morning. My father and stepmother were cocooned in their window air-conditioned bedroom watching television. Neither wanted any part of the hot humid Baltimore weather.

Securing the family car was normally a long tedious exercise involving some sort of house or yard work detail compromise. On this day the heat was so formidable that the keys were tossed my way with no verbiage or strings attached.

It wasn't long before my brother and I were on the road picking up our friends. Within minutes, the wagon had a full compliment of excited Northwooders perspiring on the vinyl seats. Having ownership of a vehicle for a day was a rare event. The restricted boundaries of walking and bike riding were shattered. A car opened up the world beyond the community. It provided empowerment.

In a car one could whistle at girls without fear of retribution. One could temporarily forget his yesterdays and tomorrows and humiliate teenagers on foot and bicycle with impunity. A car for a day, even a station wagon with an obstinate steering wheel, was a rare prize indeed.

We decided that our first stop would be lunch. Ameche's drive-in became the top vote getter. Ameche's was the place to be seen on a Friday or Saturday night. During the day, it reverted back to a fast food establishment. But we knew that at Ameche's we could stay in the wagon while the food came to us. None of us really wanted to vacate the vehicle this early on. We were all secretly afraid that once out of sight the Ford would cease to exist or maybe become a Schwinn bike.

We ate our burgers and fries quickly. Sitting in a parked car was not a lot of fun and, on top of that, the older patrons of the drive-in were glaring at us menacingly. This was their time at Ameche's and we were intruding on it.

We decided that after lunch we would cruise the winding scenic curves of the Loch Raven Reservoir. Later we'd head to 36th Street in Baltimore in a community called Hampden. Ben, who was occupying the back seat passenger window spot, swore of a news outlet there that didn't mind teenagers looking through the Stag and Adam magazines. First, the serene and majestic roads and waters of Loch Raven awaited.

As I pulled out of the drive-in, Hank, who sat in the middle rear seat between Ben and Jon, announced forcefully that he needed to use the bathroom. When the suggestion was made that he use the one provided by the drive-in establishment, Hank nixed the idea. As he held his cramping sides, he informed us of a bad experience he had there several weeks ago. The traumatized look on his face discouraged us from pursuing the topic further.

Hank insisted that we travel, without further delay, back to my house, where a less threatening bathroom resided. None of the other wagon's occupants wanted to go back there. Steve and I suspected that by now our dad might be having second thoughts about the *no strings attached* key toss and was probably at this very second pacing the living room carpet in frustration.

Hank however was adamant in his choice of toilet location. The fact that by now he was breaking wind on a regular basis sealed the deal. The bliss of a peaceful Loch Raven outing was quickly replaced by strange noises coming from Hank's body and shouts of "Oh no! Not again!" from the back seat.

We arrived at the house in record time. Everyone vacated the wagon the instant it became stationary. Hank ran up the front steps and into the house without slowing down. I often think what could have happened had our front door been locked.

We all knew that, at some point, we had to enter the house also. At the very least, some sort of explanation would be required.

The house was quiet when we went in. Hank was obviously already in the upstairs bathroom. We all stood in silence thinking that maybe, just maybe, we could make it though this unscathed. Then the toilet started flushing.

The first flush sounded like thunder in those muted surroundings. Then, in rapid succession, came more flushings. Soon the pipes within the walls began to protest their abuse. They groaned in unison to their open-air counterpart. The entire house had suddenly become a mini sewer treatment facility.

We stopped counting the flushes at ten. No longer concerned with stealth, we proceeded to take out our anger on Hank's weak bowels. Then the smell hit us. It was an odor of such monumental proportions that it sent us racing en masse to the front porch. At the same time, I heard the door to my father's bedroom slam shut. He must have opened it earlier in curiosity.

Now I knew that we were doomed. My dad would certainly take back the car keys after this fiasco. Each flush pounded more nails into my coffin. I might never feel the weight of the wagon's steering wheel again.

The minutes slowly passed as we paced on the front porch. Then, after what seemed like an eternity, Hank emerged through the door. He walked as if both his legs were broken. He was so slow and deliberate that he could have easily been eighty-five years old instead of fifteen.

Our thoughts of anger quickly turned to pity but before we could put them into words, he addressed us. It seemed that when he vacated the bathroom he had left an article of clothing behind. His underpants still resided in the upstairs lavatory.

I told Hank that despite his obvious discomfort, he needed to retrieve his underwear. Our friends Jon, Ben, and George found humor in this statement but my brother and I both saw far reaching consequences in this latest strange development. We wanted to be certain no evidence was left at the scene of the crime. Hank, however, was determined not to return to that place of bad memories. He made an offer of one dollar to any one of us who would perform the underwear rescue.

As I look back on it, I'm willing to bet that Hank would have went up to five bucks, but before he could utter another word, Ben took him up on the offer.

We looked at Ben as if he were crazy. A dollar was good money to us back then, but who knew what horrors lay waiting at the top of the stairs. It was entirely possible that both my father and stepmother were being asphyxiated as we spoke.

We pleaded with him not to do it, but he would not be deterred. Ben hurriedly mapped out a strategy. He approached the cherry tree in our front yard and snapped off a branch a couple of feet long. Then he took off his t-shirt and wrapped it about his face until only his eyes were exposed. He was ready for his mission. We all wished him well and, if memory serves, someone gave him his last rites. Hank, who knew the fate awaiting his friend, gently gripped his shoulder and said "May God be with you".

Time passed slowly as we sweated out Ben's return. When the front door finally opened, we saw the underpants first. They preceded Ben by the two-foot length of the branch. What was on the end of that stick no longer resembled underwear. They were not only discolored but also appeared ripped and torn. The smell, even outdoors, was close to unbearable. Ben had a dazed look in his eyes, as if he had witnessed a horror beyond description.

Without saying a word, Ben marched the remains of Hank's underwear to the storm drain by the street curb.

They went into the dark along with the branch. Then Ben unwrapped the shirt from around his face and tossed that in too. I'm sure only his modesty prevented him from disrobing completely.

Hank, whose discomfort outweighed his pride, asked me to take him home. He advised me that he would require the entire back seat, as he could no longer sit and needed to lie down on the vinyl.

This was no problem for the other guys. In fact, Ben had already started walking back to his house, his dollar reward long forgotten. The wagon had lost its earlier appeal. Now it simply held bad memories.

I reluctantly took Hank home, purposely running over every pothole I could find.

I discovered the extent of the damage when I arrived back at my house. I was right about my father's anger. My stepmother told me afterwards that the only thing that saved them was the air from the window air-conditioner, which they took turns breathing in.

The bathroom itself was a battlefield. Tiny round brown holes pockmarked the tile floor, the enamel of the bathtub and, yes, even the ceiling. My stepmother succeeded, with much elbow grease, in eliminating some of the marks, but the holes stayed. She later remarked that it was like someone sprayed acid in there.

As for my father, he did take back the keys. He, and my stepmother, took the wagon out for a long time. When they came back later that evening, he was in a better mood and had even brought back a pizza for my brother and me.

When I left home for the Army three years later, many things inside my house had changed. New wallpaper

154

adorned the walls in some rooms, fresh paint covered others. Some downstairs furnishings had been rearranged or replaced and the basement had a new carpet. But the upstairs bathroom had not changed a bit. All the tiny holes, compliments of Hank, in the floor, tub and ceiling were still there and I'm sure are still there today.

THE RELAPSE

A good hangout was crucial when growing up in the 1960s. It was a place where teenagers could congregate away from the eyes and ears of irritable parents. The Northwooders were fortunate to have an excellent location for hanging out; the patio in front of Northwood School. Though it was only a short block from my house, my parents never once sought me out there. It was as if that short city block had made me and my brother Steve invisible to them.

The only problem with the patio was that it was outdoors. That was no problem during the sunny warmer months, but not great on rainy or cold days.

One of our neighborhood friends, Jerry, who lived adjacent to the patio, approached Steve and I one summer morning with the idea of hanging out in his basement on dreary days. Jerry's idea was to transform his basement into a club of sorts. He would provide the drinks and the entertainment.

We both voiced our concern about his parents. It was a known fact among the Northwooders that basements were unreliable as hangouts. Parents, particularly mothers, always found reason to journey below ground when young people were gathered there. If girls were involved, dirty clothes, previously ignored, suddenly needed immediate washing. It was at those times that washing machines in perfect working order the day before, now began making noises strange enough to require a mother on stand-by just in case.

Jerry assured us that would not be the case with his folks. He promised that no clothes would be washed during his club's hours of operation, and no one of drinking age or above would be allowed on the premises.

The idea intrigued us. The patio offered little shelter from the elements. The part of it that was undercover, by the school's front doors, often acted as a wind tunnel, during particularly violent rainstorms, resulting in a group of us dashing from corner to corner while desperately trying to stay dry. An alternative bad weather site would prevent those embarrassing occurrences that the occupants of warm dry cars driving by found so amusing.

After clearing it with his parents, Jerry came up with this game plan. He would transform his basement into a clubroom setting. His idea was to imitate the folk music clubs, which were popular back then. Folding chairs would be placed about the basement room. Jerry's record player would be brought down from his bedroom along with assorted albums and singles. Jerry also had an acoustic guitar which he planned on breaking out when the mood was right.

He decided to call the club The Relapse and, with the help of his mom, made up a wooden sign with that name engraved on it. The sign was hung from the light over his basement door, which served as the entrance to the hangout.

A week before the grand opening, Jerry gave a few of us fliers to distribute to the guys in the neighborhood. The fliers proclaimed that The Relapse would be open for business the following Saturday.

A combination of curiosity and rainy weather drew a small crowd of young men to Jerry's basement that first day. There was some skepticism among our group when we noticed a sign on the basement door announcing Jerry would be performing folk songs throughout the day. Our friend Bob claimed to have heard him singing and playing his guitar a few weeks prior and found him to be "pretty crappy".

Nevertheless, we made our way into the dimly lit basement. The basement was divided into two rooms. The back room was used for storage and had a Lionel train garden set up at its center. The front of the basement was finished off as a club room with a couple of sofas, some chairs, and plenty of knotty pine on the walls.

Jerry had added to the atmosphere by stringing multi-colored Christmas lights across the drop ceiling. Posters of Bob Dylan and The Beach Boys adorned the walls. Record albums and singles were spread conspicuously around the perimeter of the room. A record player in a dark corner played *The Times They Are A Changin'*.

Jerry mingled about, guitar in hand, greeting each of us. He seemed to relish his role as the proud proprietor of the establishment. He took great pains to personally assure each one of us that his parents were forbidden from setting foot in The Relapse during its hours of operation. He hammered this point home by occasionally shouting at his folks to quiet down when he heard them walking above our heads.

With the meddlesome parents question resolved, we were all ready to enjoy some good music and conversation. But, as turned out, Jerry wasn't quite finished with his mother and father.

He had just quieted us down to make an announcement and as he began to speak, a member of his family once again had the audacity to walk the floor above us. Jerry swung into action. He ran up the basement steps in a frenzy, opened the door, and laid into his mom and dad. His tirade was such that it shook us up a bit. None of us assembled in The Relapse would have ever thought of yelling at our parents like that. But whatever he said to them worked. We did not hear a peep from either of them for the rest of the day.

That matter settled, Jerry stopped the record player and called for silence to announce some Relapse rules. Naturally, we complied. You could have heard a pin drop in the place.

Jerry began reading from a sheet of paper in his hand.

"Rule number one. No food or drinks will be allowed in The Relapse unless they are purchased on the premises."

"Rule two," he continued. "There will be no cursing or shouting on the premises. Ill mannered behavior will result in suspension of your Relapse privileges."

At this proclamation, our friend George loudly said, "you've got to be kidding!" George, who was known throughout the neighborhood for his extensive vocabulary of cuss words, had inserted a choice one between *be* and *kidding*.

Jerry wasted no time in enforcing his second rule. Though by now it was raining rather heavily, George was shown the door. His graphic opinions of the Relapse rules could be heard for a brief time between the rumbles of thunder.

Jerry reentered the room with the smug confidence of one who knows how to handle troublemakers. Counting his parents, he was now three for three on that count.

"Lastly," he said. "Anyone who steals anything from The Relapse will be beaten up then banned from the premises. This includes anything from the back room, particularly the train garden."

A couple of months earlier, Jerry had a few of us over. The next day his father noticed that the caboose was missing from his Lionel train set. Jerry was surly for several days after that incident and we naturally assumed that one of us gathered in The Relapse was long overdue for a butt whipping.

Confident that we were properly intimidated, Jerry proclaimed The Relapse as being officially open. As a group, we breathed a collective sigh of relief. The reading of the rules appeared to be over, at least for now, and Jerry had wandered into a corner, more interested in tuning his guitar than policy enforcement.

This gave us the opportunity to mingle and quietly discuss Jerry's somewhat psychotic behavior. A few seconds later, Jerry validated our concerns by breaking into a disturbingly off-key rendition of *Surfer Girl*. Though no of us would admit it, we all wondered what we had gotten ourselves into. We tried to discuss the various excuses we might use to exit The Relapse, but Jerry's warbling voice had the odd effect of numbing our brain cells.

Jimmy, who had just seen the movie *The Great Escape*, provided evidence of our collective brain freeze by suggesting that we tunnel our way out. We were in agreement that shouting out a profanity seemed to be the surest means of a quick exit, but none of us could

160

remember which rule involved getting beat up. By now, we had a feeling, they all did.

Jerry, thankfully, forgot the lyrics before the halfway point of the song. He strummed his guitar for a bit then asked for requests. "Shut up" Ben whispered next to me.

Bob, who had a fondness for Broadway musicals, requested "anything from *The Music Man.*" Jerry shook his head. "How about *Camelot?*" Bob persisted. "How about *Blowing in the Wind?*" someone yelled out. Though I assumed this question was directed toward Bob, Jerry quickly began playing the first verse of the Bob Dylan song.

Jerry's lack of song lyric knowledge eventually did him in. He seemed to realize, at the same moment I did that *how many times can a man sit down before they call him a man* was not the verse that Dylan wrote. He abruptly ended the song and threw a Kingston Trio album on the record player.

The Relapse's grand opening ended not long after that. It turned out that no acts of desperation were required to leave Jerry's basement. Jerry's recently chewed out father became our savior when he politely told Jerry from the top of the stairs, that his Aunt Sarah and her son Joey had just arrived.

Joey must have been a real handful, because when his name was announced Jerry's eyes got big and he gasped loud enough to hear over *Tom Dooley* on the record player.

Jerry began brushing us toward the basement door.

"You guys gotta leave now." He said in a shaky voice that had genuine fear in it.

Somewhere above our heads, someone began to yell Jerry's name loudly. The voice didn't sound entirely human. It had an animal quality to it that we couldn't place until much later, at the patio, when Ben said Joey's voice sounded like a goat.

In any case, it scared the hell out of us and we tore out of there as if the devil himself was chasing us.

We did go back to The Relapse again. You would be justified to ask why. Please remember that boys of a certain age have short memories, especially when the place in question is a certified *parents free zone*. Jerry assured us that Joey was back in whatever cage he escaped from, and his parents were once again humbled and avoiding creaky floorboards.

Jimmy was the first to notice a cooler resting against the far wall. Its lid held the following message: **All sodas 25 cents each. Pay first**. Jimmy opened the cooler to see several cokes, a few Dr. Peppers, and a couple of Royal Crown Colas. After his initial reaction that there was no way RCs should be the same price as cokes, Jimmy took offense at paying for something that all parents provided for free. Upon questioning Jerry on the refreshment price tag, he was given a stern look and told that The Relapse was an entertainment establishment and such places charge for drinks. Jimmy knew enough to assume that sarcasm would result in a black eye, so he held his tongue. He was determined, however, not to pay for a soda in any facility that did not stock candy and comic books.

The Relapse's second day went better than the first. Jerry had developed a sore throat, which a few of us assumed was from yelling at Joey, and passed on the singing. We listened to music and scheduled activities for the next sunny day.

The following morning was damp and chilly and The Relapse again drew a good-sized crowd. Unfortunately, the good vibes of the previous day were quickly extinguished by Jerry's obvious foul mood. It seemed that, according to our host, a coke from the previous day was unaccounted for. He had received $1.25 for four cokes and a Dr. Pepper but the cooler was short five cokes.

Jerry glared at all of us as he gave us this lesson in remedial math, but he saved his harshest stare for Jimmy. Jimmy, who rarely held back on expressing his opinion, used this opportunity to make a statement on the God given right of free sodas in a household environment.

Rather than repeat his *refreshments in a club* speech, Jerry gave Jimmy the option of leaving or getting beat up. For a brief few seconds Jimmy mulled over those two alternatives while all those assembled held their collective breath. But then Jimmy did walk out, mumbling obscenities under his breath. The majority of us were on Jimmy's side in this matter, but we knew better than to protest. The chilly winds pelting rain on the basement window dissuaded us.

Things went back to normal for the next hour or two until Jerry noticed that, once again, the recently replaced caboose from his dad's Lionel train set was missing. Then such hell broke loose that I found myself praying for the return of Joey the goat boy.

After that incident, the Northwooders pretty much lost interest in The Relapse. Dodging raindrops on the patio had become a welcome alternative to Jerry's tirades. The Relapse did remain open for a good part of that summer; though I think on most days, it was Jerry singing to himself.

I regret to say that two acts of vandalism involving The Relapse occurred between June and September. Both involved the wooden Relapse sign. At some point, a neighborhood scribe had written every cuss word imaginable on the sign in black magic marker. The sign actually stayed that way for several days until either Jerry or his parents discovered it. Though George adamantly denied responsibility for the handiwork, we all knew it had to be him. There were just too many curses, and not a single repeat in the bunch.

The second act happened after a new wooden Relapse sign was in place. One late August morning, a few of us were walking down the alley toward the patio when Ben spotted something out of place by Jerry's basement door. The Relapse sign was missing. In its place was a turkey carcass, and I mean the entire carcass, with the exception of the head and neck.

This bizarre scene held us in place for a while. Then, when someone suggested that Jerry might be home and watching us, we beat it out of there.

The turkey carcass was the final nail in the coffin for The Relapse. After it was removed, no sign replaced it and The Relapse officially closed its basement door for business. Jimmy, unlike George, did admit that the turkey was his idea. Evidently, he found it in the woods and inspiration hit. He also admitted stealing the coke. We could not get a caboose confession out of him however, and we tried our best. That was, and still is, the great-unsolved mystery of that summer.

THE GHOST DOGS OF LOCH RAVEN

Loch Raven Reservoir was a fifteen-minute drive from our Northwood neighborhood, but it might as well have been a world away. With its miles of lakes, streams, and woods, it offered a serene setting of peace and tranquility close to the concrete world we knew.

The main attraction of the reservoir was its dam. In our youth, we could walk out on an open observatory at its crest and feed the giant carp that gathered there for breadcrumbs.

Sometime in the 1970s, it was decided that, despite the hungry carp, the walkway was a safety hazard and it was cordoned off. But there were other activities to indulge in. Fishing was popular either by boat or on the shoreline. There were areas for picnicking and camping, and even skeet shooting.

My brother Steve and I would often travel to the reservoir in an attempt to capture a painted turtle or snake. We discovered that painted turtles never ventured close enough to shore to grab, and the only snake I almost snagged was a poisonous copperhead. Thankfully, of the two of us, my brother was of a sounder mind, and convinced me to let the snake go. He correctly assured me that there would be many other opportunities to harm myself in the years to come.

However safe and familiar the environment was by day; at night the reservoir became a mysterious and spooky place.

After dark, the main road that curved around the water was a haven for daters looking for a suitable parking spot. There were many such spots around the perimeter. Those of us seeking other adventures would travel off the beaten path to one of the many small side roads that dotted that area.

On one such thrill seeking evening Steve and I, and two friends, came upon a paved road that became gravel as it approached the reservoir. We found that even my father's station wagon, which was often used as an all-terrain vehicle, would only go so far before the gravel gave way to a tire rutted dirt trail.

We parked the wagon at the beginning of the tree-lined path and foraged deeper into the dark woods on foot. After several minutes, the trail ended and we found ourselves in a partial clearing. To our right a sandy cove ran into a large lake. To our left was a boggy expanse of tall reeds and dead trees. A footpath cleaved the muck.

Upon unanimously deciding to follow the path to its end, we formed a straight line and slowly made our way along the narrow divide. It was a treacherous walk. The moon was full that night, but a hazy ground fog enveloped the swamp. We could barely see a foot in front of us. On top of that, the footpath became narrower as we went along. We knew that the slightest misstep would take us into the tall reeds and the mud that fed them.

We were about to retrace our steps to the main trail when the fog mysteriously disappeared. It enabled us to view our surroundings. We were indeed enclosed by swamplands but ahead of us, and to our left, a patch of

166

land rose from the bog. On that dry piece of land, illuminated by the moonlight, a small graveyard stood. From our vantage point we could see several tombstones randomly scattered about.

Our curiosity aroused, the four of us decided to try to get closer to the old misplaced cemetery. We continued down the now more visible path until we came to the graves.

The graveyard was in a chaotic state. The tombstones were old and, for the most part, tilted at odd angles. Weeds and other strange vegetation called the dark site home. Vines, perhaps from nearby trees, had wrapped around a few of the gravestones, even lifting one a few inches off the ground. Someone lit a match and put it to one of the stones. The engraving was worn and muddy and I do not recall the name of the deceased, but I remember the date of death as 1862. The light from the match unfortunately also revealed that a couple of the graves had been tampered with.

In the center of the graveyard, two of the old markers faced large deep holes.

Though no one admitted his fright, none of us would venture closer to those dark shafts.

Then one of our group yelled and pointed towards the woods that fringed the swamp. The mist was returning, rolling in with a vengeance. In front of it, appearing to lead the way, were erratically moving yellow lights of different shapes and sizes.

That was all it took for us to beat it out of there. I would like to tell you that our retreat was deliberate and organized, but it was not. We stayed ahead of the lights and fog but paid the price in humility and mud.

All four of us stopped at the sandy shoreline cove to catch our breath and gather our thoughts. The mist drew up at the swamp's edge and we could no longer see the strange moving lights.

We decided that the most prudent course of action would be to head back up the trail to the car. Any reflecting on what we had just seen could wait until we were back on the road, with car doors tightly locked.

We split up into two pairs and headed back. No one said a word during the walk. The old gravel road was an uphill hike and my friend and I found that before long we had fallen some distance behind my brother and his pal.

Off in the distance we heard the barking of several dogs. The barking was faint and far enough away that we didn't think much of it. But as we continued to walk, the barking seemed to grow nearer. Within seconds, the barking became loud enough to believe that a pack of wild dogs were rapidly descending on us.

We both began to run but, in the dark, I tripped on a rock and landed face first in the dirt. My buddy wisely continued on without looking back.

As I lay there frozen, the barking became loud enough to know, without looking up, that the dogs had surrounded me. I honestly thought that at any moment I'd be torn apart by the ravenous beasts. Then the barking stopped. It just stopped all at once. There was abruptly no noise in those woods louder than my heartbeat.

I cautiously got up and looked around. When I saw that I was alone, I brushed myself off and hurried up the hill.

Upon my arrival at the parked car, I breathlessly blurted out my encounter with the vanishing dogs. My brother and his friend claimed to have heard nothing and my buddy backed my story by simply saying, "Yeah, I heard something too." Ultimately it was determined that my ghost dog story came in a distant second to the haunted graveyard tale.

As time went on, the friend who walked with me began to have his doubts about the entire ghost dog incident. He decided that it was either a couple of stray dogs whose frenzied yapping, echoing off the water, sounded like many more, or maybe just a flock of traveling geese. The mind can only take so much unexplained mystery.

A couple of weeks later, during the daytime, we went back down that trail. The swamp and its narrow path were still there, though, in the sunlight, much less foreboding.

We found no sign of the graveyard however. We walked the path to where we remembered it, but it was not there. We couldn't even find the elevated patch of ground where it stood.

A group of us did go back down that dirt road one evening. It was the night before my friend Dave and I were to report for enlistment in the U.S. Army. We brought our girlfriends along and hung out at the sandy cove drinking warm beer and cheap wine by the light of the moon.

We had made a vow, the four of us, not to tell anyone else about the incidents of that earlier summer night and we kept that promise.

On that warm July evening in 1966, the memories of all our adventures remained unspoken. Instead, we talked of things to come, of faraway lands and bonds that would never be broken.

At the end of the evening, in a quiet moment as we readied ourselves for the walk back to the cars, I took my future wife's hand and we looked out on the calm moonlit lake. Somewhere in the distance, we heard the splash of a fish breaking the water's surface.

But the ghost dogs remained silent.

FRIENDS AND BROTHERS

Sometimes good things come from misery and heartbreak. When my parents divorced in the late fifties, my brother Steve and I were told we'd spend the weekdays with my father in our original home, and the weekends at my mother's recently purchased row home five blocks away.

At the time, Steve and I were more upset about leaving our friends on the weekends than my parents divorcing. Their divorce didn't particularly bother us. They had been fighting for as long as we could remember. Separation was undoubtedly their best hope of not sustaining a major injury, and my brother and I seriously needed some peace and quiet.

Under normal circumstances, five blocks would not have been much of a barrier between friends, but as I said earlier, the Northwood woods divided the two communities. For some odd reason, the woods might as well have been the great wall of China. Several of our friends simply lacked the ambition to cross it and were left behind each Friday through Sunday.

It didn't take me and Steve long to find new companions on my mother's side of the woods. For some odd reason, there weren't as many kids over there. Maybe it was because it was a more established neighborhood and most were approaching adulthood.

Whatever the reason, playmates were few and far between.

Because it was an older neighborhood, there were plenty of trees and bushes to provide hiding places for games and general mischief. The steep hills of the nearby woods provided some nice sledding trails in the winter and lots of places to get lost during the warmer months.

Eventually, as we got older, most of the guys from both communities got together and formed one big, constantly revolving gang.

The boys from both communities got along just fine together. We were, after all, Northwooders, no matter which side of the woods we called home.

Steve and I felt good knowing we were the catalyst that brought all of us together. With our new friends, we were now able to play baseball with not only a catcher but a right and center fielder, and tackle football was much more enjoyable with the cushion the extra bodies provided.

The original group of Northwooders lasted until the summer of 1966, when the military draft, summer jobs and steady girlfriends came into the picture. Then, for some of us, came college, full time employment and, of course, marriage.

By the late sixties, the last of us had moved out of our old neighborhood. It was a great place to grow up, but didn't have a lot to offer us as adults. That's the way of things. What you cherish as a boy, and crave as a teenager, becomes trivial as you age. The magic is lost in the dust of the years.

A few years ago, Steve and I went back to Northwood with our wives. We found that much of it looks the same as it did so long ago. But something seemed missing. Northwood now feels like a dream that thinks it is real.

It's sad in a way, but it won't keep me from returning there from time to time. Northwood haunts me in the way a perfect memory should. It will always be part of my life.

GOING BACK

It's springtime in Northwood. A few chilly days lie ahead, but today a warm breeze blows through the old neighborhood. Summer is coming, the wind seems to say, here's a sneak peak.

We will start our journey in the parking lot of the St. Matthew's Church. It seems appropriate to begin here. The Ferris wheel of the yearly August carnival was not far from where we stand. At its crest, if the night was clear enough, and most were back then, you could see large parcel of Northwood spread out in front of you, the section we'll be traveling through today.

One might say that Northwood unofficially starts here. We rarely walked much further than the church, unless we were going to Dave's house a couple blocks up. But by then most of us had access to cars.

The sidewalks of busy Loch Raven Boulevard are close by, but the alleys draw us, as they always did. We walk down the short alleyways that connect the streets. It doesn't take long to reach the house where my brother and I grew up.

The house occupies the intersection of the alley we travel and the longer span running the entire block behind our former home. That alley, which appears to have no end, is now dotted with cars and even driveways where small fenced-in backyards once stood.

Once, in a time long ago, street vendors on wagons driven by horses, roamed these concrete channels selling their wares. Children learned to ride bikes in their narrow confines and played hopscotch and handball between the fences, always without fear of a car horn interrupting their games.

But we won't talk of things that were (well, maybe a little). We've reminisced enough in the previous pages. Today is just a pleasant walk in the sun, through places worn but unbroken by time.

Our backyard looks much smaller than it did when Steve and I played there, but otherwise seems about the same. The young tree, planted in the front yard shortly before we moved in, is now large enough to shadow most of the grassy slope along the alley side of the property.

We walk on, but pause to look down Burnwood Road. Ben once lived a couple of blocks away in that direction, as did Bob and Denny. We cross the street and pass Jimmy's house on the left. Northwood School looms ahead. There the alley ends as the school property takes over. And yes, the patio is still there, directly in front of us. Political correctness has finally caught up with our old haunt. A handicap ramp now splits its center.

Let's pause for a moment and sit on its cool curved stones. Our journey has just begun but if we're ever to reflect on what once was, this is the place to do it. In this hallowed circle we can feel the presence of our younger selves, talking about girls and planning that day or night's adventure. On the patio everything seemed possible, and the summers lasted forever.

If you feel younger while sitting here, even just a little, then you too know the magic of the place.

Now we take to the hills of the school, onto the grassy space where we once played football. Watch for thumbtacks. A few old rusty ones may still dot the ground here and there.

The last hill takes us to the road that separates the school from the woods. The rear patio, our partially enclosed foul weather alternative, is directly behind us. From our vantage point, we can see that the rear of the school, where the yearly fair was held, is now fenced in and used for parking. We can't resist trying to access the school's rear door. We are curious to see if the out of place piano still resides in the old gymnasium. But the door remains as tightly locked as it did everyday, except for one, in the summer of 1964.

You'd be right to say the woods isn't the safe refuge it once was, but we'll head for it anyhow. It is daytime after all and we're a fairly large group. We'll be safe enough for now.

The sharply inclined hill of our youth has thankfully eroded into a more graceful pitch. It is negotiated with ease. We are surprised to see that the trail leading to the stream remains the same. It's not as shocking to come across the swamp on our right. The Northwood woods swamp, the final resting place of many a cherry bomb laden model battleship, looks forlorn and desolate and scarcely holds the wonder it once did.

The clear sound of water rushing around rocks has sent most of our group toward its source, but I linger for a moment. A bullfrog, disturbed by our commotion, has begun to bellow. It is a sound as despairing as the swamp itself, but on this day it makes me smile.

When I arrive at the stream a few minutes later, I see that a few of our assembly have already made it across to the bank on the opposite side without getting wet. At one time, long ago, that would have been a rare achievement, but today the stream runs shallow. The years have managed to sap the strength of this once mighty beast. But, even weakened, it still runs fast and true.

We follow the current through the heart of the woods. The hill on our right, which leads through the trees to the street, is sharper than before. Erosion has taken its toll. We're okay with that. That section of the woods was never our favorite.

We walk on and soon the trees part to reveal a flat barren field. We named this desolate region the undiscovered country when we first found its hiding place many years ago. We take a brief detour to explore one last time this ancient plain of rocks and clay in search of fossils and arrowheads.

We join the stream near the old bridge once used by carriages and cars before the two lane highways made it obsolete. The sewer pipe that Mike and I crawled through is still there, and brackish water still trickles out of its dark gaping mouth.

We decide to exit the woods here. The stream and trees still extend as far as the eye can see but we never ventured much beyond this point. This parcel of land we owned, those woods, beyond the bridge, belonged to other young adventurers.

I am familiar with this street on the opposite side of the woods. The house my mother called home, and where Steve and I spent many a weekend, is a short walk from here. As we head back in the direction of Loch Raven Boulevard, we pass close to Hank's former residence. Further up the street is Mike's childhood home, his front yard the staging ground for many a game of tag.

Now, for a change of pace, we skip the alley and hit the sidewalk that runs up the boulevard.

To our left is the small stream where long ago I found a huge snapping turtle. When I realized, after nearly losing a thumb, the prehistoric reptile had a foul temper, I released it back to its home waters. I wonder now if it still lurks there, its anger intact, waiting for another boy with an appetizing thumb.

We cross Cold Spring Lane. The Medical Center is to our right. That pharmacy, home of the world's best vanilla malted milk shakes, is long gone, along with Jimmy Wu's Carry Out, home of the "NO FWENCH FWIE!" man.

We walk by the Northwood Appold Rec where Gene Pitney sang of heart breaking love and Miss Tilly imparted wisdom and reprimands at the fellowship circle.

Four Blocks later, we arrive at the Northwood Shopping Center. The Arundel, Reads, The Hecht Co., and The Northwood Theater are all gone as we knew they would be.

Jon lived a couple of blocks from here. We would sometimes meet him in front of the Reads Drug Store, which is currently a Laundromat.

We'll rest here for a bit, outside of where the movie theater once stood. There was a time, many years ago, when we never stopped, even briefly. In those days, the years were as light as air. They did not weigh heavy on us as they do now. In those days, much like today, we suspected our time in Northwood was short. We knew that one day we would step aside for another group of boys who wanted their time in the woods, the ball fields, the shopping centers, and maybe even the patio.

We knew we would see changes as we walked. We expected them. This journey was not about the present but the past. We passed through this place, many years before, and stayed awhile. This time our visit is brief. But, then again, it is a warm spring day in Northwood. Chilly days may lie ahead, but today is still young, the breeze is at our back, and more adventures await.

If it's true that we all live in the stories that we tell, if it's true that in those pages we are young again, then today we are ageless.

CPSIA information can be obtained
at www.ICGtesting.com
Printed in the USA
LVHW052315261118
598362LV00006B/357/P